od's prescription

r a healthy marriage and family

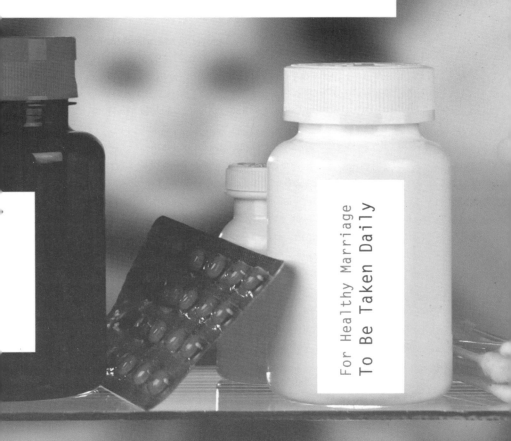

For Healthy Marriage
To Be Taken Daily

ndrew Oliver

Day One

© Day One Publications 2007
First printed 2007

ISBN 978-1-84625-095-8

British Library Cataloguing in Publication Data available

Published by Day One Publications
Ryelands Road, Leominster, HR6 8NZ
☎ 01568 613 740 FAX 01568 611 473
email—sales@dayone.co.uk
web site—www.dayone.co.uk
North American—e-mail—sales@dayonebookstore.com
North American—web site—www.dayonebookstore.com

Cover design by Wayne McMaster
Designed by Steve Devane and printed by Gutenberg Press, Malta

Across Europe, and, indeed, the Western world, the crisis in marriage and family life is impacting Christian and non-Christian alike, and Andrew Oliver's book provides a timely reminder of God's good purposes for us. His approach is thought-provoking and uncompromising and, while you might not agree with every application, you will benefit greatly from this refreshingly direct and practical introduction to what the Bible teaches.

Jonathan Lamb, Author, Director of Langham Preaching (Langham Partnership International) and former Associate General Secretary of IFES.

Commendations

Commendations

God's prescription for a healthy marriage and family **3**

Commendations

Dedication

This book is dedicated to my parents, Bertie (now deceased) and Cassie Oliver,

for providing me with a secure and loving family environment throughout all of

my childhood and adolescent years, and for teaching me so much by their

example.

Also to Ela, Rakela, Emma and Jack, the family God has entrusted to me.

Acknowledgements

This book began as a series of messages in the Rruga e Paqes (Way of Peace) church in Tirana, Albania, and I would firstly like to thank my spiritual family there who so readily received those messages. It is with a sense of indebtedness that I also express my sincere thanks to friends who have taken the time to read my manuscript and have offered much encouragement and practical advice for its improvement. To name a few: Pastors Harry Dowds and Stephen Curry, Jonathan Lamb and Ned Spiecker. In particular, I want to thank Pastor David Luke for his patience in reading my rough notes before they could even be called a manuscript. Lastly, I owe a great debt to my wife Ela, who so patiently bore with me as I spent many hours in my study working and reworking the text.

Contents

At the turn of the millennium I read a book called *A Help to Domestic Happiness* by John Angell James, first published in 1833. This book had a profound influence on my thinking on family issues from a biblical perspective. As I reflected on how most in our day approach their duties within the family, I became aware that the teaching espoused by John Angell James is much needed today. With that in mind I began to teach a series on the subject in the Rruga e Paqes (Way of Peace) churches in Tirana, Albania, during the winter of 2000–2001. There is very little by way of originality in the following pages. As will be seen by the number of quotations from various scholars past and present, the thoughts gathered here are largely borrowed from others. Nevertheless, they have proved extremely helpful to me and to the people of Rruga e Paqes churches. It is my sincere prayer that they may also prove to be a rich blessing to all who read this small book.

It must be emphasized that this study does not pretend to deal with the subject exhaustively. Many questions of detail that find no answer here may occur to the reader; but all such questions should be taken honestly to the Throne of Grace, with the confidence that God will assuredly lead the honest seeker who searches the Scriptures to know his will.

It is my belief that the family is close to the heart of God and that God's eternal and unchanging Word has much to say on the subject. The aim of this book is not to suggest and seek to answer every question that might arise. My aim is basically twofold: firstly, I want to emphasize the importance of turning to the Word of God for answers on the important subject of how to lead one's family as God intended. Secondly, I want to give an indication of and introduction to the teaching of Scripture on this fundamental area of all of our lives.

In days when parents are increasingly giving over to the state the responsibility of disciplining their children, and homes are being bombarded by immoral images of the 'family' through the television screen, the great need is for us to return to biblical principles on the family. No one can understand the mind of man greater than the One who created man. The Bible is God's manual for people created in his image.

In drawing together the final text, decisions had to be made as to whether the material should be aimed at pastors and teachers in the church or presented in such a way that it is accessible to the widest possible audience. In attempting to do both I have relegated to endnotes many of my references to the original Hebrew and Greek in which the Bible was originally written. Longer quotes from theologians of the past, including details of sources, may also be found in the endnotes. In doing this it is hoped that I have made the main text more accessible to every believer, and at the same time given enough source referencing in the endnotes for pastors and teachers to be helped in further study on this most important of subjects.

While much help can be found here for all regardless of ethnic or religious background, it is my sincere belief that true harmony within a family will only be found when each individual within that family is in a personal, harmonious relationship with God himself. The first step in achieving such harmony is to accept the Bible's teaching that we are sinners estranged from God. We need to repent of our sin and believe that the blood shed by Jesus Christ on the cross is the only sacrifice that God accepts. Any other sacrifice, including our best efforts, will never please God if we have not accepted Christ as our Saviour. For those readers who are saved, it is well to remember that remaining sin in us will continue to cause problems. Therefore I encourage you to seek God's help by consciously and consistently praying for your family.

My desire for you, the reader, is that the God of all grace will help you to have a harmonious family life.

Andrew Oliver

God is the architect of the family

A father of the fatherless and a judge for the widows,

Is God in His holy habitation.

God makes a home for the lonely;

He leads out the prisoners into prosperity,

Only the rebellious dwell in a parched land (Psalm 68:5–6).

Marriage: A convenience or an inconvenience?

The story is told of a woman who awoke during the night to find that her husband was not in bed. She put on her dressing gown and went downstairs. He was sitting at the kitchen table with a cup of coffee in front of him. He appeared to be in deep thought, just staring at the wall. She saw him wipe a tear from his eye and take a sip of his coffee.

'What's the matter, dear? Why are you down here at this time of night?' she asked.

'Do you remember twenty years ago, when we were dating and you were only sixteen?' he asked.

'Yes, I do,' she replied, remembering fondly.

'Do you remember when your father caught us kissing?'

'Yes, I remember.'

'Do you remember when he threatened me and said, "Either you marry my daughter or you spend twenty years in jail"?'

'Yes, I do,' she said.

He wiped another tear from his cheek and said, 'You know … I would have got out today.'

This humorous story reflects how, for some people, marriage or family life is simply an inconvenience. At best, some jokingly say, it is the lesser of two evils. For others it is simply a man-made invention and a convenient way of safeguarding their property.

Engels' theory

In 1883 Friedrich Engels, a close associate of Karl Marx, wrote a book called *The Origin of the Family, Private Property and the State*. According to Engels, the family originated from a primitive form of communism. He taught that human society was originally made up of promiscuous 'hordes' of people who mated indiscriminately. However, he said, as men began to become more independent and began to claim or own private property, they needed a family to whom they could pass on their inheritance. This, according to Engels, explained how the family came into being, and indeed this was the officially sanctioned theory in the former Soviet Union.[1]

The family unit in crisis

Although very few anthropologists accept Engels' theory today, in many instances it would appear that society in general treats marriage and the family as though they were invented in a cave around a flickering fire by a group of previously promiscuous cavemen. It is exactly this mindset that has created a crisis for the very existence of the family as we know it.

Millions of young people in the West seem disillusioned with conventional marriage, and are experimenting with lifestyles different from those of their parents. Many young men and women have decided to live together without the commitment of marriage, and are raising children in that context. Others do enter into the marriage relationship with a sincere desire that it is for life. They know only too well that many marriages have failed or are failing, and yet their genuine belief is that their marriage will be different because they really love each other and their love will last for ever. Then, having entered into marriage with perhaps a very limited understanding of what love really is, their marriage runs into trouble. In other words, many young people understand 'love' merely in the restricted sense of 'romance'. Real love between a married couple certainly includes romance and mutual affection; but the Bible teaches that even when one does not *feel* in love, true love practised by both partners will actually deepen and increase despite, or perhaps even as a result of, difficulties (see, for example, 1 Corinthians 13). Sadly, when the first real crisis arises in the relationships of many couples, even of those who enter marriage with the highest hopes and expectations, they opt for the easiest way out and it's off to the divorce courts. 'I could never trust him/her again' is their main plea. Little or no consideration is given to God-glorifying reconciliation. In this sense, their commitment to marriage is only partial.

This mindset can be seen in the fact that the number of divorces is on the increase every year. For example, in the United States in 1960 there were 25 divorces for every 100 marriages; in 1975 the number was 48, in 1990 it was approximately 60, and in the present day the number of divorces is closer to 65 for every 100 marriages.[2] These figures show an increase of more than 150% in one generation.[3] In 2003, the number of divorces granted in the United Kingdom increased by 3.7 %.[4]

And yet, here is the paradox. 'Over the past thirty years a consistent 96% of the American public has expressed a personal desire for marriage. Only 8% of American women consider remaining single ideal, a proportion that has not changed over the past twenty years. Even 81% of divorced and separate Americans still believe that marriage should be for life.'[5] Other surveys carried out some years ago by the Institute of Life Insurance found that 87% of the people they questioned over twenty-nine years of age chose a 'happy family life' as the most important aim in their lives.[6] This raises some very important questions: How can a young couple achieve a happy family life? What can a young man and woman do that will help them be successful in their marriage? What can they do to help them develop a healthy, happy family life together, to help them develop a secure environment in which to raise their children, in an atmosphere in which both parents are lovingly committed to serving each other's and their family's needs?

Let me begin by saying that there are no magic formulae. When we are ill and visit the doctor, we do not expect the doctor to wave a magic wand and suddenly make us better. What we do expect is that the doctor will prescribe a cure, that he will give us a prescription which, when taken, will help us to become healthier and stronger again. Alternatively, it has often been said that 'prevention is the best medicine'. In this book you will come to see that the only prescription for a healthy marriage and family life is that found in the Bible. The Bible also offers the best possible preventative medicine for life.

Remove the cultural blinkers

The challenge that we face in our day is to consider, seriously and intelligently, a prescription for the family that is firmly rooted, not in the mindset of modern Western culture, but in the Bible. I suspect that those of you who are Christians will agree with me on this point. However, in the course of these studies it is possible that even your ideas are going to be challenged. But remember: one of the reasons that the family is in crisis today is because too many people have pushed the Bible aside and have given way to and accepted contemporary thought. Biblical ideas about the family are rejected because people think they are out of date.

I am sure that, on television at least, you have seen how workhorses are blinkered. The owner puts blinkers on the horse so that it will not be distracted or frightened by things going on around it. In many ways it is possible for us to put on our own cultural blinkers and to see only what our culture has to offer in relation to marriage and the family.

The challenge to us is to put off these cultural blinkers and see what God has to say to us on this very important matter. What we need in our day is a God-given appreciation of the fundamental importance of what the Bible has to say about the family, and a dependence upon the Holy Spirit to enable us to put into practice what we learn. In summary, the prescription for a healthy family life is to put into practice biblical principles under the leading of the Holy Spirit.[7] In this chapter I want to stress just one very important principle. Although it is basic and simple, it is nevertheless fundamental. It is this: God is the architect of the family.

God is the architect of the family

In considering this point it is necessary to look at a number of foundational passages on the family. The first is found in Psalm 68, where we read in verse 6, 'God makes a home for the lonely.' Commenting on this verse, the Puritan theologian Matthew Henry says, 'When families are to be built up he is the founder of them ...' But what does this mean? Matthew Henry goes on to suggest that God brings into company those who would otherwise be lonely, and that he brings into a settled and relaxed environment those who would otherwise be unsettled. He brings into a secure environment those who would otherwise feel threatened.[8]

Chapter 1

By way of illustration, let me ask a few questions. Have you ever been alone in your home late at night? Have you ever experienced that insecurity of wondering just who is loitering in the hallway of the apartment block? Have you ever experienced that fear when every sudden noise makes your heart jump? Isn't it wonderful that God's ideal for us is that we live in the secure environment of the family? What a difference it makes when you have the company of your family with you in the house! You barely even hear those noises that would otherwise startle or frighten you. God places the solitary in families. Contrary to contemporary opinion, families were not invented by cavemen who thought it might be a good idea. From the very beginning God recognized that it was not good for man to be alone, and so placed him in the context of a family.

It is of course true that some people prefer the privacy of living alone. Others who would prefer to live with company, and enjoy the sense of belonging and security that that brings, are compelled for different reasons to live alone. However, as a general principle, God in his wisdom recognized our need for companionship and placed our first parents (Adam and Eve) in the context of a family relationship.

Secondly, we read in Genesis 2:18, 'Then the LORD God said, "It is not good for the man to be alone; I will make him a helper suitable for him."'

It is interesting that, as we read the creation narratives, at the end of each day's work we find this phrase: 'and God saw that it was good'. In all the things we read that God created, there was just one thing of which God said 'it is not good'. He said, 'It is not good for the man to be alone.' As Adam began to function as God's representative on earth, as he began his first job, that is, to name the animals, it would appear that God caused Adam to become very aware of his own solitude, and the fact that of all the animals in the garden none made a suitable helper or companion for him. So what did God do about it? Well, God places the solitary in families. First God created the individual man, the high point of all his creative acts, man made in his own image, with reason, conscience and will. Then, from the very substance of that which he had created, from the living tissue that made up man's body, God created an exact counterpart for him.

On bringing this new partner to the man, God tells them to rear a family. In Genesis 1:28 we read, 'And God said to them, "Be fruitful and multiply."'

Here is the account of the first family and of the first marriage, a marriage that was officiated at and consecrated by God himself. God is the architect of the family.

It is impossible to consider the Bible's teaching on the family in abstraction from marriage. Despite the effects of the Fall and our inherent sinfulness, in God's mind marriage and the family are inseparable. With that in mind we can see two very important things that the Bible teaches us about marriage.

MARRIAGE IS A 'PRE-FALL' INSTITUTION

We have all heard jokes about marriage. Some of them are harmless enough, but others can be as sharp as a knife. The way people sometimes talk about marriage, you would almost think it had been invented by the devil himself. Indeed, when we see how some marriages degenerate into war zones, where wives are often brutalized and beaten by their husbands (and occasionally a husband is beaten by his wife), it is understandable how some people might indeed think this way.

As mentioned earlier, some may view marriage as the lesser of two evils. In other words, marriage is bad enough, but living alone is even worse. However, marriage is not the lesser of two evils. It is not a curse. In fact, marriage was ordained by God before sin ever entered the world, before man fell into sin. It was a pre-Fall institution. Marriage is good. It was given because it was not good for man to be alone; it was given to man as a blessing.

In Genesis 2:21–25 we read of the first ever marriage and the basis for all family life. There we read how God made a woman for Adam so that he would not be lonely and that they might enjoy the physical intimacy associated with starting a family. That this passage provides the foundation for marriage and family life is clear from verse 24: 'For this cause a man shall leave his father and his mother, and shall cleave to his wife'. The man was to leave the comfort of his parents' home for an even stronger union with his wife. That this was a harmonious relationship in a perfect world untainted by sin can be seen in verse 25, where we are told that the man and the woman 'were both naked and were not ashamed'. Clearly implied in this phrase is the fact that the couple were totally at ease with each other. There was no fear of exploitation.[9] Sadly this harmony was shattered when

Chapter 1

Adam and Eve first sinned. Nevertheless, the integrity of marriage and the institution of the family were the perfect creations of God in a perfectly created world where sin had not yet entered. It was in this perfect pre-Fall setting that God placed the previously solitary Adam in a family.

MARRIAGE IS A COVENANT

The second aspect of family life we shall consider is that marriage is a covenant. There are two very important passages that demonstrate this point. The first is Proverbs 2:16–17, where we read, '… to deliver you also from the strange woman, from the adulteress who flatters with her words; that leaves the companion of her youth, and forgets the covenant of her God.' The second is Malachi 2:14 where we read, 'Yet you say, "For what reason?" Because the LORD has been a witness between you and the wife of your youth, against whom you have dealt treacherously, though she is your companion and your wife by covenant.' While there are some who think that both these passages refer to God's covenant with Israel, they nonetheless have application to the marriage covenant between a man and a woman. In that context we find in the first passage a warning from God against the adulteress who flatters with her words and leaves her husband. In doing so she is accused by God of forgetting and breaking the marriage covenant. Let me ask you a question: Whose covenant does she break? The answer, of course, is that she breaks the covenant of her God! This is clear in the second passage also, where we read that the Lord has been witness to this covenant.

What does this teach us? It teaches us primarily that marriage is a covenant made in the presence of God. Simply stated, a covenant in Scripture is the most solemn and binding arrangement into which two people can enter. All of this has very serious implications for much of modern thinking and practice. For example, marriage and the family are not man's invention, but God's perfect plan for the only creature made in his image. Therefore, we cannot treat marriage as we please. We cannot start it, use it, abuse it, stop it or change it as we please. If we are to have successful and happy marriages, marriages that please God, then we must apply God's prescription to that which is God's perfect plan for us. Covenants were terminated by death, therefore the ideal for the marriage covenant is that it too should only be terminated by death.

Secondary implications include the biblical teaching that sex outside of the marriage covenant is wrong. Whether that is adultery (sex with someone other than your own married partner) or fornication (sex before marriage), it is still wrong. As we shall see later, homosexual 'marriages' are also wrong. God's plan is marriage between a man and a woman. This is explicit in other passages of Scripture but is implicit in the passages we have just considered (see further comments in Chapter 3).

In days when society at large is turning its back on God's ideal for something as fundamental as the family, Christians need more than ever to recognize and hold fast to God's prescription for a healthy family. Young couples should be very careful not to go into marriage lightly. They should not enter marriage as though it were a test that they may or may not pass. The marriage covenant should never be ended simply because one partner thinks that he or she no longer loves the other.

Let me close this particular chapter by reaffirming that God is the architect of the family. In any building project, the architect is always available to help the builders understand his plan. God, the architect of the family, is always on hand to help his children build strong and healthy families. In building programmes many are tempted to 'cut out' or avoid using an architect, on the grounds that architects are extremely expensive. To that suggestion a wise man once responded, 'If you think good architecture is expensive, try bad architecture.' It may seem like unnecessary hard work to try to discern the Architect's advice for your family, but to press on without a healthy plan could prove very costly indeed. May it be the desire of all of our hearts to seek the Architect's advice, and avoid making unnecessary and costly mistakes in such an important area of our lives.

Study questions

FOR DISCUSSION

1. Why do you think so many couples are disillusioned with conventional marriage and choose to live without that commitment?
2. What do you see to be the main challenge facing us today regarding

Chapter 1

marriage?

3. What expectations do you and your partner have from marriage? What part do you think culture plays in your expectations?
4. What does Psalm 68:5–6 teach us about marriage and the family?
5. What do Proverbs 2:16–17 and Malachi 2:14 teach us about marriage and the family?
6. What is the basic meaning of a covenant?

FOR PERSONAL REFLECTION
7. How much do you look to God for direction for your family life?

Notes

1 *Encyclopaedia Britannica*, 'Family and Kinship: Engels' Theory', Multimedia Edition CD 1998.
2 According to **Teresa Castro Martin** and **Larry L. Bumpass,** 65% of new marriages fail ('Recent trends in marital disruption', *Demography*, 26:1 (Feb. 1998), pp. 37–51).
3 'The American family', *US News and World Report*, 27 October 1975, cited by Christenson, p. 16.
4 See statistics as recorded at: http://www.statistics.gov.uk/cci/nugget.asp?id=170
5 *Rebuilding the Nest: A Commitment to the American Family*, **David Blankehorn** (ed.), **Steve Bayme** and **Jean Bethke** (Family Service America, 1990), pp. 97–98. Cited by Christenson, p. 16.
6 'The American family', cited by Christenson, p. 16.
7 'The American family', cited by Christenson, p. 23.
8 **Matthew Henry,** *Commentary on the Whole Bible*, vol. 3 (Macdonald Publishing Company, n. d.), p. 484.
9 **Allen P. Ross,** *Creation and Blessing: A Guide to the Study and Exposition of Genesis* (Grand Rapids: Baker Book House, 1988), p. 127.

Foundations for the family in Genesis

Then the LORD God said, 'It is not good for the man to be alone; I will make him a helper suitable for him' … So the LORD God caused a deep sleep to fall upon the man, and he slept; then He took one of his ribs, and closed up the flesh at that place. And the LORD God fashioned into a woman the rib which He had taken from the man, and brought her to the man (Genesis 2:18, 21–22).

How firm a foundation?

Since the collapse of communism and the resulting open market, Albania has seen many changes. One such change is in the number of new buildings, apartment blocks and office towers that are being built. I have watched with interest as the building contractors have moved into our neighbourhood and have begun to build a new apartment block. I have observed how they have dug down perhaps three to four metres in preparation for the hundreds of cubic metres of concrete that will make up the foundations. I have also watched with interest as some buildings that have also been built over the past few years are being torn down by order of the government. They claim that such buildings have not been built to proper specification, and that in many cases the foundations were weak and therefore the buildings were in danger of collapse.

The lesson is very simple. In any building project the foundations must be appropriate to the building that will stand upon them. The same principle is true for those who desire to build healthy marriage and family relationships.

In Chapter 1 we began to consider a biblical basis for the family, especially the principle that God is the architect of the family. Now, we know that when an architect has completed his plans the next vital stage in the building process is to lay solid foundations. I emphasize that the foundations must be solid because if they are weak, then no matter how beautiful the building may appear, it is in serious danger of collapsing. In this chapter I want to continue to look at the biblical basis for the family. In particular I want to lay some foundations for the family from Genesis 1–2. The important thing to remember about what these passages have to say on the family is that the principles found here are creation principles, or, to put it another way, they are pre-Fall principles. These are principles that God gave to man before sin entered the world, before man could start to build with the bricks of cultural conditioning and the mortar of self-centredness.

This means that these are perfect principles. They were part of God's original design and plan for man and woman from the very creation of all things when God himself testified to his creation being good. So, although the rest of Scripture has much to say on the subject of the family, it is all built upon the foundational principles that God has laid down in Genesis 1–2. So what are those principles? Well, we find the first in Genesis 1:27.

THE IMAGE OF GOD SHOULD BE REFLECTED IN THE FAMILY

And God created man in His own image, in the image of God He created him; male and female He created them (Genesis 1:27).

According to this verse, man and woman were created in the image of God. Therefore, I think it is reasonable to assume that somehow the image of God should be reflected in the family. Now, it is obvious that we do not live in the Garden of Eden. Eden with all its perfection was lost when Adam and Eve sinned, and with that sin the image of God in mankind was seriously damaged. However, as Christians we have a duty to try to rediscover the image of God, firstly in ourselves, and secondly in our family relationships.

What, then, is the image of God? Let me begin by saying that there are no easy answers to that question. Furthermore, I have no intention at this point of spending time outlining the various theological ideas of the 'image of God'.[1] But allow me to give you just a couple of quotes on the subject. The first is from Sinclair B. Ferguson, who for many years was Professor of Systematic Theology at Westminster Theological Seminary in Philadelphia. He says, 'The doctrine of the image of God is the foundation for human dignity …'[2] In other words, it is the foundation upon which we are to build our honour and respect both for ourselves and for others. John Calvin gives a very practical understanding of the image of God in man in his *Institutes of the Christian Religion*. He points out that this doctrine should bear fruit in how we treat everyone, including those who hate us or try to harm us. According to Calvin, it is recognizing the image of God in others that will cause us to forgive them their transgressions and 'allures us to love and embrace them'.[3]

But isn't it interesting that more often we are guilty of the very opposite? As James points out in that well-known passage on taming the tongue, we use the tongue to bless God and at the same time to curse men who are made in the image of God. The point is that this is a glaring contradiction. We cannot praise God and yet slander men, because when we slander men we actually profane the name and image of God.

Now, let's apply this principle to our family relationships. Recognizing that each member of our family bears the image of God, we are to develop ever-increasing honour and respect for our family members. It should 'allure' us to love and embrace them, even when we don't agree with them. It should cause us to love and embrace them, even when they hurt our feelings. The Christian who will pray to and praise God with eloquent words, and yet at the same time use abusive language against a wife or husband or other family members, is living in a state of hypocrisy. It is sinful and contrary to God's design that we should treat our spouses or families with such contemptuous use of the tongue.

Of course, this applies to more than abusive language. Some people have the ability to cloak the most damning and abusive expressions in the cleanest, most pious language, and in the most pleasant manner, never losing control of their emotions. Such 'pleasantries' are equally condemned by James. God's plan is that the recognition of his image in us will cause us to have an ever-increasing respect for one another.

There is a second side to this coin, which can be seen as we reflect on the image of God in the Trinity. The Scriptures teach that God is one, and yet within the Godhead are three distinct persons. As Stuart Olyott says, 'The Father is not the Son. The Son is not the Holy Spirit. The Holy Spirit is not the Father. Each one is all of God. But each is distinct from the other.'[4] Each of the three persons of the Trinity has his own will, and yet each person does not seek to honour or glorify himself but rather seeks to glorify the others.

On this point, let's consider a few verses in the Gospel of John.

Jesus answered, 'I do not have a demon; but I honor My Father, and you dishonor Me. But I do not seek My glory; there is One who seeks and judges ... If I glorify Myself, My glory is nothing; it is My Father who glorifies Me, of whom you say, "He is our God"' (8:49–50, 54).

The immediate context of this passage is our Lord responding to the religious leaders who have just accused him of being demon-possessed. But note that Christ does not set out on a trail of self-justification. Rather, he seeks to honour his heavenly Father (v. 49) and in turn he is confident that his Father will glorify him (v. 54). On this point Matthew Henry says, 'Self-honour is no honour ... Christ and all that are his depend upon God for their honour, and he that is sure of honour where he is known cares not though he be slighted ...'[5] In John 8:50 Jesus says, 'I do not seek My glory', but rather (v. 49) he seeks to honour his Father. Why does Christ not seek his own glory? The answer is to be found in verse 54 where he says, 'If I glorify Myself, My glory is nothing.'

In the context of the family relationship, if everyone only takes from the others, seeking only his or her own good, pleasure, glory or honour, then that glory is nothing. It is the duty of every Christian above all else to love and honour God, and next to that to love our neighbours as ourselves (Matthew 22:37–39; Mark 12:30–31; Luke 10:27). When this principle is taken and applied more specifically to our family relationships, it means primarily that God should be put first and honoured in our families. He should be honoured by our admitting our dependence upon him and by our heartfelt daily thanks for all that we have. Furthermore, this principle implies that all members of the family should do all they can for the good of the others. This will involve striving to promote the comfort and happiness of the others and treating them as we would like them to treat us, with courtesy and utmost respect in all things. Our attitude should be one of giving our energies and our time for the good of the others. Jesus himself said, 'It is more blessed to give than to receive' (quoted by Paul in Acts

20:35). This is especially true within the context of the family.

Some of you may be single men, looking forward to the day when you get married. You may be thinking it will be good to have a wife, someone to cook your food, and wash and iron your clothes, someone to keep the house clean, etc. You probably think that if you are out working all day then you should not have to do any work in the house. I want to challenge that type of thinking with those words of our Lord: 'It is more blessed to give than to receive.' If you are truly seeking to honour your wife, as Christ sought to honour the Father, then at least occasionally you should be prepared to roll up your sleeves and help your wife with the housework. A young husband should be prepared to change that dirty nappy or get up in the middle of the night and check on the baby.

Husbands, when you get home from work and are feeling absolutely dead on your feet but your wife wants to talk to you about something that happened during the day, how do you react? Do you put your own tiredness first and simply ignore your wife by burying your nose in a newspaper or focusing your attention directly on the football match on television? Or, despite your own tiredness, do you put your wife's needs before your own and give her your undivided attention? Let's be perfectly honest with ourselves. The easiest thing to do is to lose ourselves in the newspaper and just pretend that we are listening to our wives. It takes effort to give our families the time and attention they need and deserve. However, the rewards will be great as you see your relationship develop, deepen and strengthen.

And you wives, the other side to that coin is that you should not place unnecessary pressure or demands upon your husband. Even with the greatest of effort to give due attention to his wife there will be times when the very thing your husband needs is a few minutes' quietness.

The key is to try to be as sensitive as possible to each other. It is important to try with all your heart to understand each other and to appreciate each other's needs. Christ's relationship with his heavenly Father was such that his greatest desire was to do his will and to please him. Are we reflecting that image in our family relationships? It is impossible to cover all eventualities or possible circumstances, and in many respects it is up to each family unit to work out the details of what is best in their own home. But remember: the general principle of Scripture applies to all, and that is that each person should seek the good of the other. This will obviously involve both doing certain things and avoiding certain other things. For example, as John Angell James puts it, 'There will be no searching after faults, nor examining with microscopic scrutiny, such as cannot be concealed; nor reproachful epithets; no rude contempt; no incivility; no cold neglect; there should be courtesy without ceremony; politeness without formality; attention without slavery; it should in short be the tenderness of love, supported by esteem and guided by politeness.'[6]

Sadly, if we are sincere at this point we all have to admit that most families and couples are far from this ideal. This simply means that we need to work all the harder at reflecting God's image in our family relationships.

THE EQUALITY OF GOD SHOULD BE REFLECTED IN THE FAMILY

That God intended man and woman to be treated as equals is clear from New Testament passages such as Galatians 3:28, 'There is neither Jew nor Greek, there is neither slave nor free man, there is neither male nor female; for you are all are one in Christ Jesus.' However, we do not have to turn to the New Testament for this teaching. God, in his wisdom, expressed it as part of the foundations that he laid in Genesis. Look again at Genesis 2:18, where God says, 'I will make him a helper suitable for him.' Unfortunately, most English translations do not express this phrase 'helper suitable' as clearly as the Hebrew.

The phrase used in the Hebrew is *ezer kenegdo*.[7] *Ezer* simply means 'helper', but the interesting thing about this word *ezer* is the way that it is sometimes used to describe God as the 'helper' of his servants. For example, we read in 1 Samuel 7:12, 'Then Samuel took a stone and set it between Mizpah and Shen, and named it *Ebenezer*, saying, "Thus far the LORD has helped us"' (emphasis added).[8] The first part of the name, Eben, literally means 'stone', and the second part, Ezer, is the same word that is used in Genesis 2:18. So, Samuel set up the 'stone of help' as a reminder that God had helped his people. Now, no one would dare say that God was inferior to Samuel simply because he was Samuel's helper. The important point is that the word *ezer* is not used to describe someone who is a slave or an inferior. At the very least, it describes someone who is an equal or even superior.

At this point the second word, *kenegdo*, tells us what kind of helper God was going to make for Adam.[9] *Kenegdo* literally means 'as in front of him' or 'according to what is in front of him'.[10] Notice what it does not say. It does not say 'according to what was above him'. That could indicate that the woman was superior to man. Neither does it say 'according to what was below him'. That could indicate that the woman was inferior to man. The woman was made 'according to what was in front of him'. This indicates absolute equality. The woman was not to be man's master, nor his slave, but his equal. Just as Father, Son and Holy Spirit are absolutely equal but with different jobs to do, so man and woman are absolutely equal but with different God-given jobs to do. Matthew Henry illustrated beautifully both the essential equality and the role distinction between man and wife when he commented on the phrase that woman was made from a part of the man's side ('And the LORD God fashioned into a woman the rib which He had taken from the man', Genesis 2:22). Henry put it like this: 'The woman was made of a rib out of the side of Adam; not made out of his head to rule over him, nor out of his feet to be trampled upon by him, but out of his side to be equal with him, under his arm to be protected, and near to his heart to be loved.'[11]

The imagery in these often-quoted words is beautiful, to say the least. It depicts a heart-warming harmony that surely every young bride desires to find with the husband of her dreams. It illustrates the union of two equals, and yet shows the man, ordinarily the physically stronger of the two, to be the protector. But how often is a young woman wooed by the gentle words and affectionate behaviour of a young man, and is full of hope and expectation that this is how the married relationship will continue, only to find that not long into married life the husband treats her as a master might treat a slave, someone designed to make his life as comfortable as possible! What a gulf there often is, due to our sin, between what God desires for us and what our relationships develop into!

After marriage a young man may be tempted to think that he has been robbed of the freedom he had to spend time with his friends, etc., but such thinking is foreign to the idea of marriage as God intended. Adam may have been tempted to think that he had been robbed of a rib, but as John Calvin puts it, '… something was taken from Adam, in order that he might embrace, with greater benevolence, a part of himself'.[12] Just as Adam lost one of his ribs but as a result was given an even greater and more precious gift, any so-called freedom that a young man may feel he has lost is replaced by the even greater and more precious gift to be found in a godly wife. In Proverbs 18:22 we read, 'He who finds a wife finds a good thing, and obtains favor from the LORD.' And again in Proverbs 31:10–11, 'An excellent wife, who can find? For her worth is far above jewels. The heart of her husband trusts in her, and he will have no lack of gain.' The far greater reward, the jewel that a young man finds in a godly wife, is that of a faithful partner for life, an equal who will cheer him in the good times and help him through difficult times that come his way. But only in treating her with the equality she deserves will a husband enjoy that reward to the full.

One might, of course, raise the issue that the woman was made to be man's helper and not vice versa, and legitimately ask questions such as: Is there not a creation order to be observed? How does this square with New Testament passages on headship? In response I will say no more here other than that, whatever headship implies in the home, it cannot mean that the husband is superior to the wife; that does serious injustice to the biblical teaching on equality. Such issues, however, will be dealt with later when we look at the particular duties of husbands and wives. For now, allow me to draw your attention to just one more foundational principle from Genesis 2.

THE WISDOM OF GOD SHOULD BE APPLIED IN THE FAMILY

And the man said, 'This is now bone of my bones, and flesh of my flesh; she shall be called Woman, because she was taken out of Man.' For this cause a man shall leave his father and his mother, and shall cleave to his wife; and they shall become one flesh (Genesis 2:23–24).

In this passage God gives us a very important principle which is often neglected. In neglecting it, young couples very often hurt themselves and their partners, and even the wider family. I am not talking here about the 'one flesh' principle, which is also very important and needs to be understood and controlled. Rather I want to look at the following: 'a man shall leave his father and his mother, and shall cleave to his wife.'

What does it mean to 'leave' and 'cleave'? This word 'leave' is very strong. It has the meaning of a very definite forsaking or abandoning, the idea of a 'clean break'. As an illustration, have you ever noticed that sometimes when you try to break a green stick, very often it is difficult to get a clean break? Although it is definitely broken, the two parts do not come apart because the twisted sinews hold them together. However, when you break a dry stick, the two parts come apart easily in your hands. This word 'leave' refers to the second type of break. It is a clean break, where both parts are very definitely separated.

The word 'cleave' is also a strong word. It is a word that has the meaning of being joined tightly, like two pieces of metal welded together. It is a strong bond. Indeed, metal workers will often say that a properly welded joint is stronger than the original metal.

What happens when a young couple decide to get married? The answer is that they agree to make the marriage relationship stronger than any other relationship they have. They make a commitment to live together as one social and economic unit and to become mutually dependent upon each other.[13] Such leaving and cleaving is absolutely essential if a young couple are to have the healthy marriage that God intended. How can I say this? Because God has said it right here in Genesis 2. Unlike so much modern thinking, the most important family relationship is not the parent–child relationship; it is the husband-wife relationship.

The parent-child relationship must be severed effectively. I emphasize effectively; this does not mean completely. In other words, this does not mean completely turning your back on your parents, never to interact with them again. Children (and remember you are always your parents' child, no matter how old you are) are to honour and respect their parents (we shall see more of this in Chapter 8). However, the relationship that a man had with his parents as a bachelor cannot stay the same after he has married. Furthermore, the relationship that a man had with his friends before he was married cannot continue the same after he has married. His time and energies must now be focused upon his new family unit. This means, for example, that decisions must be made *within* the family unit. While the advice of wise parents may be sought, the counsel of a godly wife or husband must be considered more important. To put it rather more directly, parents should never be allowed to interfere in the decision-making process of the new family unit.

This teaching has many implications. I know that in Albanian society, for example, it is often difficult for a young couple to find a place of their own to live. Therefore many couples will live in the home of the man's parents. Maybe I'm wrong, but I have never seen a kitchen that has been made for two women. Sooner or later the knives are going to fly, at least verbally! If at all possible, therefore, the leaving should be physical, even if this only involves moving into rented accommodation next door. The young couple should do all in their power to find a place of their own and the parents should help them in this.

Furthermore, the leaving should be both an emotional and a mental leaving. There is no point in a young woman sitting in her wonderful new apartment or house with her husband if she is constantly thinking about and missing her parents. This also will lead to unnecessary stress in a new marriage.

Let me leave you again with the principles of Scripture, which apply in every culture: the *image* of God should be reflected in the family; the *equality* of God should be reflected in the family; and the *wisdom* of God should be applied in the family. May God bless you with a healthy and happy family life as you seek to put these important principles into practice.

Study questions

FOR DISCUSSION

Read Genesis 1:27 and 2:18–25.
1. Why are these passages so important for a proper understanding of family life as God intended it to be?
2. What does the term 'pre-Fall' mean?
3. Why is the biblical teaching about the 'image of God' so important to a proper understanding of family relationships?
4. What principle can we draw out of John 8:49 that will help us understand how a family ought to function?

5. How might the words of Jesus that 'It is more blessed to give than to receive' (see Acts 20:35) be put into practice in your family?
6. Look at Genesis 2:18. The word 'helper' in this passage cannot mean 'inferior'. Why? How does the word 'suitable' reinforce this?
7. How do Proverbs 18:22 and 31:10 teach the great worth and dignity of a wife?
8. Read Genesis 2:24–25. What are the practical implications of this passage for a family?

FOR PERSONAL REFLECTION

9. As a consequence of the teaching in this chapter, are there any practical changes you need to make in your family life?

Notes

1 For a summary of those interpretations see 'Image of God' by **S. B. Ferguson** in *New Dictionary of Theology* (Leicester: IVP, 1988), p. 328.
2 Ibid. p. 329.
3 **John Calvin,** *Institutes of the Christian Religion*, III: vii: 6.
4 **Stuart Olyott,** *The Three are One* (Welwyn: Evangelical Press, 1979), p. 54.
5 **Matthew Henry,** *Commentary on the Whole Bible*, vol. 5 (Macdonald Publishing Company, n. d.), p. 1005.
6 **John Angell James,** *A Help to Domestic Happiness*, pp. 18–19.
7 *ezer kenegdo* (עֵזֶר כְּנֶגְדּוֹ). The Old Testament was originally written in the Hebrew language.
8 Other passages include: Exodus 18:4; Deuteronomy 33:7,26,29; Psalm 20:2; 33:20; 70:5; 89:19; 115:9–11; 121:1–2; 124:8; 146:5; Hosea 13:9.
9 *kenegdo* (כְּנֶגְדּוֹ).
10 **Victor P. Hamilton,** *Genesis*, NICOT (Grand Rapids: Eerdmans, 1991), p. 175.
11 **Matthew Henry,** *Commentary on the Whole Bible*, vol. 3 (Macdonald Publishing Company, n. d.), p. 20.
12 **John Calvin,** *Commentaries*, vol. 1 (Grand Rapids: Baker Book House, 1998), p. 133.
13 **Paul Marston,** *God and the Family*, p. 28.

Chapter 3

Finding the right partner

Do not be bound together with unbelievers; for what partnership
have righteousness and lawlessness, or what fellowship has light
with darkness? Or what harmony has Christ with Belial, or what
has a believer in common with an unbeliever? Or what agreement
has the temple of God with idols? For we are the temple of the
living God; just as God said, 'I will dwell in them and walk among
them; and I will be their God, and they shall be My people.
Therefore, come out from their midst and be separate,' says the
Lord. 'And do not touch what is unclean; and I will welcome you.
And I will be a father to you, And you shall be sons and daughters
to Me,' says the Lord Almighty (2 Corinthians 6:14–18).

You will reap according to what you sow
Every farmer knows that, if he does not plan in advance, when harvest time
comes he will have nothing to harvest. The farmer must plan in advance. He
must consider what type of crop he wants to grow and eventually harvest.
Obviously, the type of crop he wants to harvest will determine the type of
seed that he will plant. He will also give serious thought to how the ground
needs to be prepared for each crop, when is the best time to sow different
seeds, and how to avoid those seeds being damaged by weeds.

The farmer will observe his crops as they begin to appear above the
ground and eventually mature into plants ready for harvesting. It would be
a very surprised farmer indeed who set out in the spring to plant a field full
of potato seedlings, only to find that, when harvest time arrived, his field
was full of carrots! The general laws of nature dictate that whatever type of
plant the farmer sows in spring, he will reap the mature plant of those
seedlings at harvest time.

The apostle Paul uses this imagery in Galatians 6:7–8, where we read these words: ' Do not be deceived, God is not mocked; for whatever a man sows, this he will also reap. For the one who sows to his own flesh shall from the flesh reap corruption, but the one who sows to the Spirit shall from the Spirit reap eternal life.' The context of these verses is that of Christians bearing one another's burdens. More specifically (v. 6) Paul refers to supplying the needs of the one who teaches in the church.[1] However, the text may also be understood in a more general sense: that everyone, believers and non-believers, shall reap according to what they sow. For example, a non-believer cannot deny God in this life and yet expect his blessings in the next. On the other hand, the believer who serves God and obeys him will not only inherit eternal life but is actually storing up treasures in heaven (Matthew 6:19–21).

In this chapter I want to take this principle and show its relevance to the family. I want to show that what we sow during the dating period will have a significant impact upon the sort of family life that we will have. If, for example, you sow lies and deceit, or hide things from your partner while dating, then you can expect to reap a family life where you cannot trust each other. If you sow the seeds of physical and verbal abuse, don't expect marriage to change this. You will reap a home where you will try to 'win' an argument by hurting your spouse, either with words or with your fists. In any case, you will reap an atmosphere of insecurity where you and your children live in constant fear of the next disagreement.

On the other hand, if seeds of a quiet and agreeable spirit are sown while dating, and both partners care more for the other than they do for themselves, with a genuine desire to resolve their arguments according to the principles of God's Word, then they will reap an atmosphere in the home where the most difficult subjects can be talked about, and where each member of the family feels secure and loved, no matter what difficulties may arise.

Of course, this does not mean that you will have no problems. Even the best Christian homes have their problems. Even in homes where both partners have the gentlest spirit and quietest demeanour there will be times when there are disagreements. Those disagreements may be as simple as over what colour the decor ought to be in the home, or they may be over such things as how a child ought to be disciplined. The simple point is that no two minds think absolutely alike. Furthermore (and this may come as a bit of a surprise to some who are deeply in love), no matter how wonderful your partner may be, he or she is not perfect! It is worth bearing in mind that when two people (even Christians) decide to get married, it is not two angels who are getting married, but two sinful children of Adam. If you are in any doubt about this, just spend some time reading Romans 7, where we find that even the apostle Paul struggled with continuing sin in his life (see also 1 John 1:8–10).

Perhaps one of the most talked about (or at least, thought about) subjects among young people concerns whom they would like to marry and when, and this is as true of the boys as it is of the girls. Mental plans are formed as to what sort of partner they would like to have, how they might possibly arrange their home, and even how many children they might eventually have together. With this in mind, when young Christians are planning for the future with specific reference to the family, it is important that they build into those plans key fundamental or foundational principles from God's Word.

In this chapter I want to focus on a few foundational principles for the family that the single child of God should lay down firmly even before meeting a potential partner, and certainly during the dating period. It must be stressed at this point that these are only foundational *principles*. As every couple discovers, even with the most careful planning and desire to do things the best possible way, getting married takes a relationship into a whole new dimension, with many ongoing issues that will need to be resolved as they arise. We will consider these foundational principles under the general heading: How can I find the right partner?

Old Testament examples

In the culture of Bible times, it was often the parents who chose a partner for their children. However, there were exceptions to this. For example, Jacob fell in love with Rachel (Genesis 29:18ff) and chose her to be his wife (even though his father set the boundaries of his search[2]). Moses, having fled from Egypt and far from his natural and adoptive parents, obviously chose Zipporah as his wife (Exodus 2:21). Furthermore, Ruth cast her eyes upon Boaz and they eventually got married. Of course, not everyone who chose his or her own partner made a wise choice. For example, Samson's choice of Delilah was not the wisest decision he ever made.

We can learn a number of things from this. Firstly, although in Bible times the parents very often chose a partner for their children, it was not something commanded by God and there were exceptions. In other words, the Bible does not say that it is your parents' responsibility to find your partner for you. However, since parents usually have a child's best interests at heart, any advice they give should not be quickly dismissed, although one should not rush to be too compliant with parents' wishes After all it is not they who will have to live with the person afterwards. The final decision as to whom you should marry is in your own hands. It is not your parents' responsibility.

Furthermore, a parent's (especially an unsaved parent's) definition of who would make a good partner may fall well short of the criteria given by God throughout the Bible. This is the second thing that we can learn: that the Bible gives very clear guidelines for choosing a partner. According to the examples we find in the Old Testament, it is important that you should choose one who has the same religious beliefs as you have.[3] Abraham stressed the importance of this in finding a wife for Isaac (Genesis 24:3ff), and Isaac made the same point to Jacob (Genesis 28:1). What was the reason for this? Well, quite simply so that they might continue to enjoy the blessings of God, and not be lured away from worshipping the true and living God. Before entering the Promised Land God warned the Israelites not to intermarry with the people there. In Deuteronomy 7:3–4 we read, 'You shall not intermarry with them; you shall not give your daughters to their sons, nor shall you take their daughters for your sons. For they will turn your sons away from following Me to serve other gods; then the anger of the LORD will be kindled against you, and He will quickly destroy you.' For Christians today, as the children of God, it is God's desire for us to marry only other Christians.

The unequal yoke

In 2 Corinthians 6:14–16 the apostle Paul writes, 'Do not be bound together with unbelievers; for what partnership have righteousness and lawlessness, or what fellowship has light with darkness?' As John Calvin correctly points out, this verse does not refer directly to marriage[4] but nevertheless, on this principle, marriage to a non-believer will also be prohibited. The metaphor Paul uses here is taken from oxen and donkeys being yoked together to work the land. Not only was this something that was forbidden by Jewish law (Deuteronomy 22:10), it also has very practical consequences. Oxen and donkeys are very different animals. They differ in size and walk at a different pace. On a practical level, these differences will make it very difficult for them to work together.

Likewise there will be specific difficulties for the believer who marries an unbeliever. Believers have been made righteous in Christ (Romans 3:21; 5:17; 10:10; Philippians 1:11; 3:9), whereas unbelievers remain unrighteous. Believers have been made light in the Lord (Ephesians 5:8); unbelievers are still in darkness. Young people, if you marry an unbeliever you can expect difficulties in your marriage, especially in the area of your relationship with God. As the prophet Amos said, how can two people walk together unless they are agreed (Amos 3:3)? How can two people walk together through married life, unless they are agreed on this fundamental issue?

It is true, of course, that sometimes the influence of the believer will lead the unbeliever to become a Christian. I have seen this happen with friends of mine. However, this is more down to God's grace than to the believer's choice of a partner. More often, believers are drawn away from the Lord. They lose the passion that they had for serving God, and often this is because other, physical passions have been awakened and possibly indulged in, leading to a sense of guilt, shame and a desire to hide from God. And what about the children of such a marriage? Will they not be completely confused? Who are they to believe? The mother who tries to teach them according to the Word of God, but who has failed to put it into practice herself, or the father who has no time for the things of God? Remember, whatever a man sows, this he will also reap. For your own sake and for the glory of God, be careful of the foundations that you lay when choosing a partner.

At this point I feel it necessary to make a short excursion and address those who may already be married to someone outside the faith. Perhaps you were married before you became a Christian, or perhaps in ignorance or disobedience you married an unbeliever. First of all let me address the disobedient, and say that if your conscience is not bothering you about this, then it should. No true child of God with the Spirit of God witnessing in his or her heart can possibly continue unchallenged by the Word of God about personal disobedience and the need for repentance. However, rather than merely rebuke at this point, I want to offer hope. If, for whatever reason, you are married to an unbeliever, God offers hope.

In 1 Corinthians 7:13–14, Paul addresses Christians whose partners are not believers. Reading between the lines, it would appear that some Christians were thinking that they should leave their unbelieving partners. Perhaps they thought it the best way to sanctify themselves wholly to God, or that as Christians it was now wrong for them to remain married to an unbeliever. To these women Paul says that so long as the unbelieving husband is willing to stay, the Christian wife should not even consider leaving him. Such is the high place of the marriage vows in the eyes of Paul. Furthermore, Paul continues by pointing out that the unbelieving partner is 'sanctified' by the believing partner (v. 14). Now, what does this mean?

The word 'sanctified' has already been used by Paul in 1 Corinthians 1:2,30 and 6:11 to describe salvation. However, whatever it means here, it cannot mean 'saved', as it is a nonsense to talk of someone who is both 'unbelieving' and 'saved' at the same time.[5] Paul makes this clear in 7:16 when he says, 'How do you know, O wife, whether you will save your husband? Or how do you know, O husband, whether you will save your wife?' It would appear that Paul is giving the Christian partner the hope or assurance that, rather than them having been contaminated by contact with their unbelieving partners, the opposite is true. The unbelieving partner is actually in a privileged position by virtue of his or her marriage to a Christian.

John Calvin suggests that the piety or godliness of the saved partner has more potential to have a positive influence on the marriage than the unsaved partner's ungodliness has to polluting it. He points out that the unbelieving partner is not saved by virtue of being married to the believer; rather, Paul simply seems to be saying that the marriage itself still enjoys God's blessing.[6] Calvin further suggests that the unsaved partner is not in such a hopeless condition that he or she may not eventually be saved.[7]

There can be no guarantee that a Christian's godly influence will lead to the salvation of his or her partner. Salvation is strictly a sovereign work of God. Nevertheless, God uses human instruments in his plan of salvation, so in this sense he may, if he so desires, use a believing partner to lead an unbelieving partner to salvation. So long as the marriage between the believer and the unbeliever is maintained, the potential for seeing the unbeliever saved remains. As Gordon Fee puts it, 'If the husband/wife is "holy", then the unbelieving spouse is also "holy", that is, set apart in a special way that hopefully will lead to their salvation.'[8]

The hope that is offered to any Christian who is married to an unbeliever, then, is that because of the holy (godly) influence in the home, there is the very real possibility that the unbelieving partner (and children) may also come to the point of repentance for their sins and faith in the Lord Jesus Christ as the only Saviour of mankind.

'OK,' you say. 'You have told us whom not to marry, but the point you were to make was "whom should I marry?"' Well, there are some clear biblical criteria that help us in this matter.

First of all, it should be someone who is free to marry. Single men should not set their affections on another man's wife, and single women should not set their affections on another woman's husband. The Scriptures clearly condemn the adulterous relationship (see, for example, Leviticus 18:20; 20:10; Proverbs 6:26; Romans 7:3). How easy it is to fall prey to this! It often starts with something as simple as a second look, progresses to the flirtatious smile, and before you know it you have established the foundations for an adulterous relationship. In addressing this, let me remind you of the words of the Lord himself in Matthew 5:27–28: 'You have heard that it was said, "You shall not commit adultery"; but I say to you, that everyone who looks on a woman to lust for her has committed adultery with her already in his heart.'

Such a relationship does not begin with the act of physical union in some shady hotel room. It begins in the 'hotel room' of the mind through the doorway of the eyes. The first essential criterion, then, for whom we should marry is that it must be someone who is free to marry. Be careful to guard your hearts and minds in this area.[9]

Secondly, it should be someone of the opposite sex. We have already mentioned this briefly in Chapter 1 but it is worth noting that God makes this clear: 'You shall not lie with a male as one lies with a female; it is an abomination' (Leviticus 18:22). God's plan is marriage between a man and a woman. Therefore it is ridiculous to talk of homosexual couples 'adopting' and rearing children in what they consider to be a family unit. It is God alone who determines the boundaries for the family. *The Times* newspaper on Thursday, 19 July 2001 printed a short article in which it stated that the Constitutional Court in Berlin had given permission for homosexual marriages. As a result gay couples were to be allowed to register a 'life partnership' and it would be illegal to discriminate against a person in a same-sex relationship. This has widespread legal implications, especially in the workplace but also in the whole area of parenthood. But it is God who has established the family. It is he who has declared in his Word what marriage is and with whom it ought to be.[10]

Thirdly, this same passage teaches that any potential marriage partner should be someone who is not a close relative ('None of you shall approach any blood relative of his to uncover nakedness; I am the LORD ...', Leviticus 18:6–18).

Fourthly, as we have seen, it should be another Christian.

Apart from these clear criteria, the Bible teaches that we can marry whomever we like. This is taught in 1 Corinthians 7:39 by the apostle Paul: 'A wife is bound as long as her husband lives; but if her husband is dead, she is free to be married to whom she wishes, only in the Lord.'

The context of this verse is that of Paul addressing the issue of remarriage of Christian widows. Once again, the sanctity of marriage is stressed. A woman is bound to her husband so long as he is still alive. However, should the husband die the widow is free to remarry. Paul sets forth only one clear criterion for the widow's choice of a new partner. If she is to remarry, then she must marry 'only in the Lord'; in other words, she must marry a Christian. Apart from this one stipulation, the widow is free to marry 'whom she wishes'.

Now, if we take this principle and apply it to the case of the virgin mentioned in verses 36–38, then surely we must come to a similar conclusion. If Paul says that it is 'well' for the virgin to marry (or remain single if she desires), then, just like the widow, who obviously had a say in whom she married, the virgin may marry whomever she pleases so long as that person is a Christian. It appears to me that, so long as the other criteria mentioned above are fulfilled, young Christian men or women can marry the person of their choice.

Is there compatibility?

'But,' you might say, 'what if we are not compatible?' Many young people believe that to have a happy family life they must have as much in common with their partner as possible. They think that it is important that they both like the same music or television programmes, or that if they have had a university education, they must marry someone who has also had a university education. They must be compatible!

There is some truth in this. I think that in some ways it is easier for a couple who have certain interests in common. However, compatibility can also be overstressed. It is possible, for example, for two people to get married who both studied law and became lawyers, who both like to listen to Bob Dylan or jazz music, and like to walk along the beach with the wind blowing in their hair (unless, of course, he is bald). Unfortunately, although they may seem completely compatible they too could end up getting divorced. Let's remember that even though a degree of compatibility may prove advantageous, the real basis of marriage is not compatibility but commitment.

Commitment to solve your problems biblically

The basis of marriage is a commitment based on God's example of a covenant relationship. This will involve commitment to what is best for your partner as well as to talk over and solve problems together from God's Word and in God's way.[11] Other things may help, but the commitment to solve problems biblically is essential. Dr Jay Adams, who has spent many years teaching in Westminster Theological Seminary in the United States, and has written many books on biblical counselling, makes this point very strongly in a number of his books. He says, 'Steer clear of any potential marriage partner who wants to avoid solving problems … or who cannot work together with you using biblical principles to reach God-honouring answers.'[12] If you are considering a long-term relationship with someone, one of the first things you should do is see if both of you are willing and able to work out problems by applying God-given principles. If your partner is unable to do this, you should stop the relationship immediately. Then tell the other person why you have ended the relationship and do not start that relationship again unless the other person changes in this vital area.

These are difficult words, and I know that it is difficult to end a relationship with someone of whom you have grown very fond. But which will be more difficult? The heartache of ending a relationship in the early stages or that of seeing a family torn apart after you are married and have children? Even if the marriage does not end in divorce, there will always be nagging tensions in the practical area of family life between the partner who desires to raise the family according to God's Word and the partner who has no time for God or the principles he has so clearly laid down in Scripture. If there is no willingness to resolve problems God's way while dating, then do not be fooled into thinking that this will change when you are married.

By way of conclusion, let me encourage you to think seriously about the things discussed in this chapter. If you are in a relationship, let me encourage you to pray together about these things and to seek God's best for you and your partner. If you are still single, let me encourage you to pray for God's choice of a partner for you—but do not stop there. First of all, consider how Abraham sent his servant out to look for a wife for Isaac. No doubt Abraham believed in a sovereign God, but he also recognized his responsibility to do something. Consider also how, when Abraham sent his servant to find a wife for Isaac, the servant set a wonderful example of praying for God's guidance. But he did not stop there. We read that when he saw Rebekah he ran up to her. Now, can you imagine what would have happened if he had run away from her? Perhaps had he lived in this modern age he could have called her up again on his mobile phone, but even so I think his personal approach was better. Young people, when you pray 'Give me this day my daily bread', do you then sit and wait for that bread to fall into your hands? Of course not. The idea is ridiculous. Rather, you go out to earn your bread. Likewise, when you ask for God's guidance to find a partner, do not expect that partner to fall into your lap. Get up on your feet and get out of the house and go to places where Christians meet, and then approach them, befriend them, talk to them, and by God's grace you will find that someone special. May God bless you in this very practical area of your life.

Study questions

FOR DISCUSSION

1. Read Genesis 25:29–34.
   (a) In what way did Esau live for the moment, and what were the consequences of his actions?
   (b) In what ways might you see Esau's behaviour reflected in the way you make decisions in your life?
2. Read 2 Samuel 11:1–12:15.
   (a) In what way did David live for sensuality?
   (b) What were the consequences of his sin?
3. Read 2 Corinthians 6:14–18 and 1 Corinthians 7:13–14.
   (a) Why is it so important that a Christian dates (and possibly marries) only another Christian?
   (b) Make a list of the potential problems for a Christian who dates (and possibly marries) a non-Christian. Discuss the list.
4. Discuss the following:
   (a) Why do you think there are so many divorces in Western societies?
   (b) In what ways (if any) do you see this to be a consequence of modern dating practices?
5. Read Romans 12:16.
   (a) How do you think this verse might be applied to the idea of 'compatibility' in a relationship?
   (b) What do you think are the most essential elements of compatibility in a relationship?

FOR PERSONAL REFLECTION

6. Living for sensuality:
   (a) In what ways (if any) have you been living for sensuality?
   (b) What will you do to change this?

Notes

1 See **John Calvin,** *Commentaries*, vol. 21 (Grand Rapids, MI: Baker Book House, 1988), pp. 176ff. For an alternative view see **R. C. H. Lenski,** *The Interpretation of St Paul's Epistles to the Galatians, Ephesians and Philippians* (Minneapolis, MN: Augsburg Publishing House, 1937), pp. 299ff.

2 In Genesis 28:1–2 we read: 'So Isaac called Jacob and blessed him and charged him, "You shall not take a wife from the daughters of Canaan. Arise, go to Paddan-aram, to the house of Bethuel your mother's father; and from there take to yourself a wife from the daughters of Laban your mother's brother."'

3 See **Marston,** *God and the Family*, p. 34.

4 **John Calvin,** *Commentaries*, vol. 20 (Grand Rapids, MI: Baker Book House, 1988), pp. 257ff.

5 See **Gordon D. Fee,** *The First Epistle to the Corinthians*, NICNT (Grand Rapids, MI: Eerdmans, 1987), p. 299; and **Peter Naylor,** *1 Corinthians*, Welwyn Student Commentary (Welwyn: Evangelical Press, 1996), pp. 130ff.

6 **John Calvin,** 'The First Epistle to the Corinthians', in *Commentaries*, vol. 20 (Grand Rapids: Baker Book House, 1988), pp. 241–242. 'While this sanctification is taken in various senses, I refer it simply to marriage, in this sense—it might seem (judging from appearance) as if a believing wife contracted infection from an unbelieving husband, so as to make the connection unlawful; but it is otherwise, for the piety of the one has more effect in sanctifying marriage than the impiety of the other in polluting it … Meanwhile this sanctification is of no benefit to the unbelieving party; it only serves thus far, that the believing party is not contaminated by intercourse with him, and the marriage itself is not profaned.'

7 Ibid. pp. 244–245: 'Now unbelievers are not in so hopeless a condition that they may not believe. They are dead, it is true, but God can even raise the dead. So long, therefore, as there remains any hope of doing good, and the pious wife knows not but that she may by her holy conversation (1 Peter 3:1) bring back her husband into the way, she ought to try every means before leaving him; for so long as a man's salvation is doubtful, it becomes us to be prepared rather to hope the best.'

8 **Gordon D. Fee,** *The First Epistle to the Corinthians*, NICNT (Grand Rapids: Eerdmans, 1987), p. 301.

9 It is beyond the scope of this book to deal with the whole area of divorce and whether or not divorced persons are free to marry. For two views I suggest that you read: **Jay E. Adams,**

Marriage, Divorce, and Remarriage in the Bible (Zondervan, 1980); and **Andrew Cornes,** *Divorce and Remarriage: Biblical Principles and Pastoral Practice* (London: Hodder & Stoughton, 1973).

10 For the sake of clarity, I must state that I have absolutely no tendency towards homophobia, but am simply stating what is clearly taught in the Bible.

11 Adams, *Christian Living*, p. 64.

12 Ibid. p. 65.

Aids to proper behaviour while dating

Flee immorality. Every other sin that a man commits is outside the body, but the immoral man sins against his own body. Or do you not know that your body is a temple of the Holy Spirit who is in you, whom you have from God, and that you are not your own? For you have been bought with a price: therefore glorify God in your body (1 Corinthians 6:18–20).

Who's watching whom?

One day the king gave Nastradini[1] this order: 'The town is full of beggars, and they are so shameless that they follow people and won't leave them alone until they get some money. Get a notebook and a pen and make a list of these shameless people. I am going to kick them out of town.'

Nastradini got a notebook and pen, and the first thing he did was to write down the king's name. When the king saw his name on the list, he was speechless with anger. Nastradini said, 'Don't be angry, O ruler of the people. You simply gave me the order to make a list of the shameless beggars in this town. That's all I've done.'

'What are you saying?' replied the king. 'That I, the king, am a beggar? And among those that are most shameless?'

'Why are you angry, your Majesty? The sun doesn't cover us with riddles, and you are indeed among those that are most shameless.'

'So, according to you, I should be put out of town?' responded the king.

'Yes, your Majesty! The other beggars are not as dangerous as you. They take something from the people by asking, whereas you take it by force, threats and beatings.'[2]

Isn't it interesting that, when we think about behaviour, it seems that we are always quick to see the faults in others and yet fail to see what we are doing wrong ourselves! It is always dangerous to make assumptions but I think it is fairly safe to assume that one area where young couples have problems with their behaviour is with physical contact. I'm not talking about the potential for a boxing match between both partners, although I suppose it could be described as a form of wrestling!

In this chapter I want to give some biblical principles for proper behaviour during the dating or engagement period. What I do not want to do here is use unnecessarily explicit language in setting out these principles. No doubt there are occasions when this is necessary, however, in my opinion, that should take place in the privacy of the pastor's study. There are a couple of very simple reasons for this: firstly, people do not need to hear such explanations if they are not struggling with sexual sin; and secondly, to use explicit language when people are not struggling with sexual sin can actually cause them to start thinking about such things, and may even cause them to sin in their minds. Young people (including young Christians) do, however, need to be educated on sexual matters. For this reason I strongly recommend a chapter called 'The intimate life' in *No Longer Two*, an excellent book by Brian and Barbara Edwards published by Day One and designed to be used by young couples preparing for marriage.

It is difficult for young Christian couples to keep pure during the dating and engagement period. No matter how devoted two young Christians are to pleasing God, as they spend more time together and as they look forward to getting married the temptation to sexual sin will become stronger. I have heard of young Christian couples who try to overcome temptations by praying and reading the Bible together (very commendable exercises). Yet half an hour later their physical desires overtake them and they begin to do the very things that they know they should not do.

In *principle* it is this type of difficulty that Paul addresses in Romans 7.[3] In verse 19 of that chapter Paul says, 'For the good that I wish, I do not do; but I practice the very evil that I do not wish.' A more literal translation would be: 'I have the desire to do good, but I cannot do it.' In other words, Paul is saying: 'I know what I must do to please God—in fact, I want to do what pleases God—but I do not do it!' Here we have very clear reference to the fact that even the apostle Paul struggled with temptation to sin. The greatest and best-known saints of God have had their struggles with sin, just as you and I struggle with temptation to sin in every area of life, not just in relationships.

However, there is help at hand. In 1 Corinthians 10:13 we read these encouraging words: 'No temptation has overtaken you but such as is common to man; and God is faithful, who will not allow you to be tempted beyond what you are able, but with the temptation will provide the way of escape also, that you may be able to endure it.'

By way of illustration, allow me to share with you a personal incident. During our time in Northern Ireland my wife Ela was quite amused by the roads there. In the first instance Ela was amused because the roads in Northern Ireland are rarely straight. They wind and twist their way throughout the countryside. But another characteristic of the roads in Northern Ireland is that there are usually at least two routes to any destination. For example, to get to the town of Omagh from my family home in Castlederg there are three main routes, all approximately the same distance, and many other alternative routes also. Now, if one of the roads is completely blocked, due to an accident or road works, it is still possible to reach your destination by choosing another route. Indeed, one or two miles before road works you will very often see a sign that says 'DIVERSION', with an arrow pointing to an alternative route.

On reading such a sign you can do one of two things: either you can follow the direction of the sign and reach your destination by a safe route; or you can ignore the diversion sign, but sooner or later you will find yourself trapped in heavy road works, with nowhere to go but back. Since getting out of trouble is always more difficult than avoiding it, it is always wiser to follow the diversion signs. I want to show you some diversion signs in the Bible which will help you to avoid getting into difficulty in your relationship during the dating and engagement period.

BE HOLY

The first diversion sign is fundamental to all the others, and is stated by God on many occasions in Scripture. It is: 'Be holy.' The word 'holy' has the basic meaning of 'separate'. It means to be separated from sin and devoted to God.[4] Peter tells us to 'be holy' rather than live according to the evil desires we had before we were Christians (1 Peter 1:14–16). To live a holy life, then, is to live according to the principles of the Bible in contrast to the

sinful ways of the world. This means:
• Do not allow the society you are living in to dictate how you behave.
• Do not allow the culture you are living in to dictate how you behave.
• Do not allow your peers at school, university or work to dictate how you behave.
As God's children, we are to be different from the world: we are to be holy and live according to God's standards. The following 'diversions' are based on these standards.

In the Song of Solomon 2:7 we read, 'I adjure you, O daughters of Jerusalem, by the gazelles or by the hinds of the field, that you will not arouse or awaken my love until she pleases.' Based on this verse, our second 'diversion' is:

DO NOT AWAKEN PASSIONS

Contrary to popular opinion within some mainstream Christian groups, the Bible does not teach that sex is simply for producing babies. Such notions stem from the teaching of many of the Early Church Fathers (theologians in the church from around the first to third centuries) who taught that the sexual side of our natures is dirty or debased. For example, in the first century, Justin Martyr described sex as a 'lawless desire'.[5] In the second century, Tatian described physical intimacy in these terms: 'If any one sows to the flesh, of the flesh he shall reap corruption; but he sows to the flesh who is joined to a woman; therefore he who takes a wife and sows in the flesh, of the flesh he shall reap corruption.'[6] In the fourth century, Augustine wrote of the strength of sexual desire, suggesting that it is so all-consuming that it stops us thinking clearly.[7]

The Bible, however, presents physical intimacy in much more positive terms. In fact, according to the Scriptures, such intimacy is natural and healthy. Remember what we read in Genesis 2:24–25, where sexual intimacy is described as a man and woman becoming 'one flesh'. It also says that they 'were both naked and felt no shame'. Obviously this was before sin entered the world and spoiled all that God had made good. Nevertheless, according to these verses, God created sex as an expression of the deepest personal intimacy. 'This passage should dispel forever the myth that God is anti-sex or that sex is somehow part of our "lower" animal natures.'[8] The gift of physical intimacy between a husband and wife is something that brings two people closer together than anything else. It brings them together not only physically but also emotionally. As far as God is concerned this is the deepest expression of love in a relationship and 'it is good'. The Song of Solomon is another wonderful expression of God's good gift to us.

However, it is only 'good' when it is exercised within God's framework, and that framework is marriage. The Song of Solomon relates how wonderful sexual intimacy is between a man and his wife. So strong are these desires that the reader is warned not to 'arouse or awaken my love until she pleases'. On three occasions we read this warning in this book, so it must be important. It would seem that at least part of the message of the Song of Solomon is this: while love and intimacy between a man and a woman is a wonderful gift, there is a time and a place for that love to be awakened, and that time and place is only within marriage. There is a very good reason for this. Love and intimacy are very strong emotions, and once those passions have been awakened they cannot be stopped easily. According to Song of Solomon 8:7, 'Many waters cannot quench love, nor will rivers overflow it.' The lesson is simple. As single persons, do not awaken those passions. If you do, you will find yourself in a downward spiral, falling deeper and deeper into the sin of fornication. Furthermore, if your relationship does not work out you will find yourself hurt much more deeply. That is why God has set up the diversion sign which says that we should not 'arouse or awaken … love until she pleases'.

LOVE IS PATIENT
Our third diversion sign is found in 1 Corinthians 13:4: 'Love is patient, love is kind, and is not jealous; love does not brag and is not arrogant …'

To be true to the original text, it must be stated that the Greek word used here is *agape*, which refers to the self-giving love of God as revealed in Jesus,[9] and not *eros*, the Greek word for sexual love. Nevertheless, we have here a very important general principle: 'love is patient'! If you love your partner with self-giving love (that is, with *agape* love) as indeed you should, then out of love for your partner you will be patient in the area of physical intimacy and you will wait until you are married before expressing your

Chapter 4

eros love for each other.

In 2 Samuel 13:10–15 we have an example of what can happen when love is not patient. In verse 1 of that chapter we read that Amnon 'loved' Tamar. In fact, he 'loved' her so much that he became ill thinking about her. So what did he do? He made a plan so that he could sleep with her. We read:

Then Amnon said to Tamar, 'Bring the food into the bedroom, that I may eat from your hand.' So Tamar took the cakes which she had made and brought them into the bedroom to her brother Amnon. When she brought them to him to eat, he took hold of her and said to her, 'Come, lie with me, my sister.' But she answered him, 'No, my brother, do not violate me, for such a thing is not done in Israel; do not do this disgraceful thing! As for me, where could I get rid of my reproach? And as for you, you will be like one of the fools in Israel. Now therefore, please speak to the king, for he will not withhold me from you.' However, he would not listen to her; since he was stronger than she, he violated her and lay with her. Then Amnon hated her with a very great hatred; for the hatred with which he hated her was greater than the love with which he had loved her. And Amnon said to her, 'Get up, go away!'

Look again at verses 12–13. Tamar pleaded with Amnon not to have this wrong relationship with her. She even cleverly tried to escape the moment by suggesting that perhaps the king would grant permission for them to marry.[10] But even with such a prospect before him, Amnon would not wait. He refused to be patient and he raped Tamar. Then what happened? Look at verse 15: Amnon hated Tamar and their relationship in every aspect came to a very unhappy end.

The practical implications for any young couple should be obvious. Men, you have a very serious responsibility. You have a responsibility not to play with a girl's affections so that you can have some momentary physical pleasure and then leave her and move on to the next girl. This same challenge is likewise addressed to the girls, since in our promiscuous society very often the girls are as free and easy about their sexual encounters as many of the boys.

In Genesis 29:15–30 we find a wonderful example of patience in this area. There we read how Jacob worked for seven years to take Rachel as his wife, working another seven after Laban's treachery. And in all that time

Jacob did not behave indecently towards Rachel. If you really love someone, you will be patient and wait until the time is right. In other words, you will wait until you are married.

FLEE FORNICATION

In 1 Corinthians 6:18 we find our fourth diversion sign. 'Flee immorality. Every other sin that a man commits is outside the body, but the immoral man sins against his own body.'

At this point in our study let me attempt to answer the big question that almost all young Christians ask at some point in their relationship with a member of the opposite sex. That question is: 'How far?' How far can a young couple go with physical contact before they are committing a sin? On a scale of 'holding hands' to 'all the way', how far can they go before they get married? Well, to answer that question let me remind you of our second principle: 'Do not awaken passions.' This principle is very clear. If you are not married, do not awaken passions. For Christians there is no such thing as a scale to determine where sex begins. For example, let's consider kissing. A kiss can be as innocent as simply expressing affection towards your partner, and as such is healthy and acceptable. However, a kiss can also be used to awaken a partner's passions. In fact, what very often starts out as the former can quickly become the latter. I think that it is fair to say that most couples have no difficulty knowing when they are being sexual with their partners. Often the 'how far' question is simply an excuse for getting into situations where passions will be inflamed. Let's look again at what the apostle Paul says in 1 Corinthians 6:18. His advice (in the form of a command) is 'flee immorality'. Paul does not sit back and ponder, 'How far can young people go with physical contact before they are committing a sin?' Rather, he says, 'Flee immorality'! Therefore, instead of asking how far you can go with physical contact, you should be asking, 'How far can I run from temptation?'

Having made that necessary qualification, I think it is only fair to respond briefly to such enquiries as 'Is it all right to kiss my partner?' and 'Is it all right to hold hands?' The obvious answer is that so long as such practices are not being used to excite you or your partner's passions, then they are healthy enough, in and of themselves. However, to help you avoid the harmless kiss or hug deteriorating into something that is wrong, let me suggest some simple guidelines.

Avoid long periods alone in private. Do not place yourself in unnecessary temptation by spending hours together alone. Now I know that it is important for a couple to spend time alone. I know that it is important to have privacy away from family and friends. However, it is actually possible to be 'alone' in a crowd. It is possible, for example, to be 'alone' in a café or restaurant where no one knows you, or walking the promenade at a busy seaside town. In fact, you will find that a couple will often talk more and get to know each other better in such situations. Indeed, holding hands and making eye contact at such times can be very intimate and precious and does not carry the guilt of wrong behaviour.

If you do happen to end up alone in a room at home or university (something I strongly advise against), leave the door slightly open so that family or friends are free to enter the room. The fear of someone entering the room is a simple safeguard against wrong behaviour.

Guard your eyes. Be careful of what you watch on TV or read in magazines, or even how you look at someone in the street. On this point allow me to quote Augustine at length:

Though a passing glance be directed towards any man, let your eyes look fixedly at none; for when you are walking you are not forbidden to see men, but you must neither let your desires go out to them, nor wish to be the objects of desire on their part. For it is not only by touch that a woman awakens in any man or cherishes towards him such desire, this may be done by inward feelings and by looks. And say not that you have chaste minds though you may have wanton eyes, for a wanton eye is the index of a wanton heart. And when wanton hearts exchange signals with each other in looks, though the tongue is silent, and are, by the force of sensual passion, pleased by the reciprocation of inflamed desire, their purity of character is gone, though their bodies are not defiled by any act of uncleanness.[11]

Although addressed to nuns, this quote contains principles that we would all do well to apply to ourselves. Sexual passions can be inflamed by a look just as quickly as with a touch, so guard your eyes and your thoughts against such temptation. In other words, do not feed your passions. It is better to be like Job, who made a covenant with his eyes not to view women as sexual objects (Job 31:1).

Remember that even when no one else is present, God is. It is actually good to acknowledge this by spending time together in prayer and reading God's Word. In fact, a good exercise for young Christian couples is to do a Bible study together in preparation for marriage.[12] Again, this can be done in privacy while at the same time safeguarding against temptation by taking some simple measures. Such measures might include arranging to do your study in one of your families' homes where others are present (but not in the same room), leaving the door slightly ajar so that others in the home have easy access. For accountability it is advisable to do such a study under the supervision of a pastor, reporting to him perhaps once a week. The key is to think ahead and avoid placing yourselves in a situation where you know temptations may be given room to develop.

GET MARRIED

The fifth and final 'diversion' that I want to leave with you is found in 1 Corinthians 7:8–9, where we read, 'But I say to the unmarried and to widows that it is good for them if they remain even as I. But if they do not have self-control, let them marry; for it is better to marry than to burn.'

Here we have the ultimate step for the young Christian couple who are struggling with their passions. If you know that you love your partner, but those passions have been awakened, if you are finding it almost impossible to be patient, if you are constantly fleeing fornication to the point where you cannot bear the pressure any longer, then Paul has the answer to your problems: get married! Look again at verse 9. Paul is simply saying that, if you do not have self-control, if you are struggling with sexual temptation, then do not burn with passion; rather, get married.

Girls, when a boy is being very sweet with you and is trying to persuade you to do things you know are wrong by telling you how much he loves you, put his love to the test. Tell him, 'Let's get married!' Now, if he begins to look a bit ill or says that he is not ready to get married, remind him of God's Word and tell him that if he is not ready to get married, he is not ready to play intimate games. The Bible is very clear. Sexual intimacy belongs within marriage. Matthew Henry puts it like this: 'This is God's remedy for lust. The fire may be quenched by the means he has appointed. And marriage is much better than to burn with impure and lustful desires.'[13]

Of course, lack of self-control in this area is not the only reason for a young Christian couple to get married, nor indeed should it be the primary reason for marriage. Only if a young couple have a strong relationship in every other way—a good personal relationship with God, a sincere and genuine appreciation of each other's qualities and characters, a sincere and genuine desire to work out any difficulties they may have according to the Word of God—and are seriously contemplating marriage anyway, only then should temptation of a sexual nature lead them to marry possibly quicker than they had anticipated.

Paul shows this again when he advises, 'But because of immoralities, let each man have his own wife, and let each woman have her own husband' (1 Corinthians 7:2).

It has been suggested that those who cannot control themselves before marriage will probably struggle with the same sin after marriage. Perhaps as a single person you are allowing your eyes to wander and are looking at members of the opposite sex in a way that you know is not right. Or perhaps you are tempted to think, 'What harm is there in it?' or 'Who knows about it, anyway?' Well, firstly, God knows everything. You may be able to hide your sin from others, but God sees the deepest recesses of all our hearts. Secondly, such behaviour is habit-forming. What do I mean by that? Quite simply that you are forming sinful habits that, even after you are married, will prove difficult to break. If you are single and struggling with such temptations today, do not allow those temptations to develop into sinful habits. And remember that you have help: God will not allow you to be tempted beyond what you can endure (1 Corinthians 10:13).

Whatever practical measures you take, let me encourage you again to lay solid foundations for your family while dating. These will help you to build a strong God-glorifying family life in the future.

Study questions

FOR DISCUSSION
1. Read 2 Samuel 13:1–19.

(a) What evidence is there that Amnon was more infatuated, rather than actually in love, with Tamar?

(b) What was the consequence of Amnon's passion?

2. Read Romans 12:1–2.

(a) What does it mean to present your body to the Lord as a living and holy sacrifice?

(b) How can you apply this to relationships, especially dating, in your life?

3. Read Genesis 39.

(a) What were the qualities in Joseph's character that stopped him from taking advantage of the opportunity to sin with Potiphar's wife? (Read also Galatians 5:22–23.)

(b) What principles can you draw from the life of Joseph and apply to your life, especially when dating? (Read also 1 Corinthians 6:18.)

4. Read Galatians 5:19–24. In what ways should the characteristics mentioned in verses 22–23 be applied when dating?

5. Read 1 Corinthians 6:12–20.

(a) What is the relationship between the Christian's body and the Lord?

(b) Why should the Christian forsake immorality?

FOR PERSONAL REFLECTION

6. What do you think is the most important application for your life now so that you can remain pure sexually?

Notes

1 Nastradini is a character from Albanian folklore.

2 From *Nastradini: Anekdota' Enciklopedi Humor & Satirë* (Argeta-LMG, 2001), p. 217.

3 I emphasize the word 'principle' because there is no indication that Paul's difficulty was sexual temptation; the principle is, however, the same.

4 See **Jerry Bridges,** *The Pursuit of Holiness* (New Malden: NavPress, 1985), p. 19.

5 From 'Fragments of the work of Justin on the Resurrection', *The Ante-Nicene Fathers*, vol. 1, The Master Christian Library (version 2.0) (SAGE Software, 1996), p. 615.

6 *The Ante-Nicene Fathers*, vol. 2 (SAGE), p. 167.

7 **Augustine,** *City of God*, from *The Nicene and Post Nicene Fathers*, vol. 2, The Master

Christian Library (version 2.0) (SAGE Software, 1996), p. 599. 'So possessing indeed is this pleasure, that at the moment of time in which it is consummated, all mental activity is suspended. What friend of wisdom and holy joys, who, being married, but knowing, as the Apostle says, "how to possess his vessel in sanctification and honor, not in the disease of desire, as the Gentiles who know not God," would not prefer, if this were possible, to beget children without this lust …'

8 **Payne** and **Jensen,** *Pure Sex*, p. 21.

9 **J. P. Baker,** *New Dictionary of Theology* (Leicester: IVP, 1988), p. 398.

10 What Tamar was suggesting was in fact against the Levitical laws with reference to marriage between stepbrothers and sisters. However, I agree with Keil and Delitzsch when they suggest that Tamar simply said this 'as Clericus observes, "that she might escape from his hands by any means in her power, and to avoid inflaming him still more and driving him into sin by precluding all hope of marriage."' Cited by **Keil and Delitzsch,** *Commentary on the Old Testament* (Eerdmans, 1991), vol. 2, p. 399.

11 *Letters of Saint Augustine*, from *The Nicene and Post Nicene Fathers*, vol. 1, The Master Christian Library (version 2.0) (SAGE Software, 1996), p. 1149.

12 I recommend **Brian and Barbara Edwards,** *No Longer Two: A Guide for Christian Engagement and Marriage* (Epsom: Day One Publications, 1994).

13 **Matthew Henry,** *Commentary on the Whole Bible* (Macdonald Publishing Company, n. d.), · vol. 6, p. 537.

Reciprocal responsibilities of husband and wife

Husbands, love your wives, just as Christ also loved the church and gave Himself up for her … So husbands ought also to love their own wives as their own bodies. He who loves his own wife loves himself (Ephesians 5:25, 28).

Get real!

The story is told of a wife who suddenly took ill and died. Her husband dutifully arranged the funeral, and many friends and relatives came to say their last goodbyes. As the coffin was being carried from the upstairs room, those performing the duty came to a corner on the stairs. As they turned the corner the coffin bumped against the wall, and to everyone's amazement the wife sat up in the coffin, alive and well! Twenty years later the wife died again, and again the husband dutifully performed all the necessary arrangements for a fitting funeral. As the helpers were carrying the coffin out of the upstairs room and approached the same corner against which the coffin had bumped twenty years earlier, the husband discreetly urged the carriers, 'Be careful, please, and don't bump against the wall!'

This rather humorous story reflects the sad fact that many marriages degenerate to the point where some husbands and wives simply stay together out of a sense of duty, and when death comes to one partner the other is actually glad to be freed from the marriage commitments. A sense of duty is a good thing in a marriage, but marriage can be much more fulfilling when it goes beyond the realms of duty to the point where even duties are carried out with a strong sense of wanting to please the partner. Such an approach to fulfilling responsibilities is inevitably made much easier when it is reciprocated. In other words, marriage does entail the fulfilment of responsibilities and commitments, but if those responsibilities are carried out by both partners as God intended, they engender that respect and love which constitutes a healthy marriage.

Martin Luther once said of marriage: 'Ah dear God, marriage is not a thing of nature but a gift of God, the sweetest, the dearest, and the purest life above all celibacy and all singleness, *when it turns out well*, though the very devil if it does not' (emphasis added).[1]

It is my firm conviction that if we are to have marriages that 'turn out well', to use Luther's terminology, then we need to get real and seriously consider what responsibilities are involved in marriage according to the Scriptures. This is what I aim to do over the next few chapters, looking firstly at the reciprocal responsibilities of husband and wife, and then moving on to consider separately the special responsibilities for wives and husbands.

What do I mean by 'reciprocal responsibilities of husband and wife'?[2] To put it very simply, I mean those duties or responsibilities which must come from each partner. They are responsibilities which a husband must perform 100 per cent towards his wife, and at the same time a wife must perform 100 per cent towards her husband. They are responsibilities which must be mutually carried out if a family is to function as God desires.

What, then, are these reciprocal responsibilities? The first, which is the foundation for all the rest, is:

LOVE EACH OTHER

In Ephesians 5:25 we read, 'Husbands, love your wives …' Now, although this is a responsibility which is applied to the husband in a special way (as we shall see in Chapter 6), nevertheless it is equally the responsibility of the woman to love her husband. In the home, love must be mutual otherwise it will be a very sad home indeed. I don't think that I am exaggerating the point if I say that there can be no real happiness or contentment in a home where love is not mutual. I believe that God in his wisdom recognizes this and so he also gives a special injunction to young wives. In Titus 2:3–5 we read:

Older women likewise are to be reverent in their behavior, not malicious gossips, nor enslaved to much wine, teaching what is good, that they may encourage the young women to love their husbands, to love their children, to be sensible, pure, workers at home, kind, being subject to their own husbands, that the word of God may not be dishonored.

Look again at verse 4: 'Encourage the young women to love their husbands.' While God gives a special command to husbands to love their wives, yet he recognizes that love must be mutual or there can be no true happiness in the home.

At this point it is appropriate to make a brief excursion and consider the nature of love according to the Bible. A key passage in understanding the biblical concept of love is, of course, 1 Corinthians 13. Although in 1 Corinthians Paul is addressing the church and the love that Christians ought to have for their fellow-believers, the Greek word used there is *agape*, the same word used in Ephesians 5:25 to describe the love husbands are to show to their wives.[3] *Agape* love is patient, kind, not jealous, not boastful and not arrogant. It is never rude or selfish, and does not seek to 'get even'. The apostle Paul's idea of love is one of seeking the good of others rather than selfishness.

But there is another aspect to biblical love, and we find that expressed in Titus 2:4, where Paul uses the word *philandrous*, meaning 'husband-lovers'.[4] This word is based on the Greek word *phileo* (love) which has the idea of tender affection.[5]

In the Old Testament the most common word for 'love' is the Hebrew term *ahabah*.[6] This word has a very broad usage. It often refers to the love of one person for another in a general sense, and it sometimes refers to God's love for his people, or a man's love for a woman. It is also this word that is used to express sexual love, frequently used, for example in the Song of Solomon.[7] This is clearly the idea behind Paul's exhortation: 'Let the husband fulfill his duty to his wife, and likewise also the wife to her husband' (1 Corinthians 7:3). Gordon Fee says, 'The sentence emphasizes two things: (1) that sexual relations are a "due" within the marriage [v. 3] because (2) the body is not one's free possession but belongs to one's spouse [v. 4].'[8]

So then, when we talk of love between a husband and wife, we are referring to the type of love that embraces all three of these concepts: *agape* love, with all that is associated with that particular term, the tender affection of *phileo*, and finally the sexual expression of love as found in the Old Testament term and behind Paul's comments in 1 Corinthians 7. In other words, the love of a husband for his wife, and of a wife for her husband, should encompass the more objective sense of duty, the self-sacrificing service and commitment to one's partner, and the more subjective feelings-orientated aspect of tender affection and sexual desire.

It is possible that many marriages run into difficulty because young couples enter marriage with little more than the subjective, romantic, affectionate understanding of love. It is important that young people are made aware that often such a restricted idea can in fact blind one's eyes to the difficult, and sometimes painful, realities that arise in the course of married life.

In ordinary cases,[9] how can there be true happiness if there is not the reciprocation of such love? Firstly, there can be no happiness for the person who does not love. Why? Well, imagine for a moment being tied to a person for the rest of your life for whom you have no loving feelings. Imagine sitting down to breakfast every morning for the rest of your life, looking across the table to face someone who brings no warmth to your heart or smile to your face. Imagine every conversation being one of necessity rather than an open sharing of your inner fears and concerns, and your affections being poured out upon your children because you have no outlet for your affections with your partner. Even from these few examples it is clear that there can be no happiness in a family for the person who does not cultivate love for his or her partner.

Secondly, there can be no happiness for the person who does love! Why? Because where love is not being reciprocated it must surely wither and die, just as a flower must die that is starved of the rain and sunshine which bring it warmth and vitality! If love under such circumstances does not wither and die, at the very least it will become a mere duty to be fulfilled. As mentioned above, duty certainly has its place in the marriage relationship,[10] but love in its fullest sense between man and wife, as God intended it, is surely much more rewarding and fulfilling.

What sort of family life can you have without reciprocal love? 'One that functions,' you might answer. That is true; a marriage can 'function' under such circumstances, but not as God intended it to function, with mutual warmth and compassion, and an open expression of love such as we read of in the Song of Solomon. This being the case, couples, young and not so young, should do all in their power to guard their love for each other so that nothing is allowed to dampen, or indeed destroy, such love. Be careful not to quench love, especially in the early years of marriage when 'little faults' are being recognized. I think it is fair to say that, whatever knowledge a couple gain about each other before marriage, it is never so accurate, comprehensive or illuminating as that which they gain by being married and living together twenty-four hours a day.

By way of illustration, let me ask this: have you ever had a small thorn in your finger, so small that you could barely see it? If you have, you will know that if it is not removed it can cause what is initially a very small wound to become a much larger and much more painful running sore. In the same way, small defects in a person's personality or behaviour may be overlooked while dating, but in the more intense relationship of marriage, if they are not dealt with appropriately they can become 'running sores' which dampen love. Small offences or hurts against your partner can be overlooked for a time, but they have the potential to build up and cause a lot of unnecessary pain to every member of the family, and can stifle and dampen love, especially in its early growth.

To illustrate this further, allow me to draw from the world of botany. I'm sure you know how a small plant, when it first breaks forth from the soil, can be easily damaged by the slightest wind. However, as it grows and draws vitality from the earth and energy from the sun, it becomes stronger and can even eventually withstand storms. In the same way, when a husband and wife are given time to grow in their relationship they can better withstand any difficulties that may arise. For this reason, couples should fuel their love for each other by removing the fuel from any disagreement. In other words, they should avoid prolonged arguments. In Ephesians 4:26–27 we read, 'Be angry, and yet do not sin; do not let the sun go down on your anger, and do not give the devil an opportunity.' Look again at verse 26: 'Do not let the sun go down on your anger.' A man and his wife should be careful to extinguish arguments the same day that they begin.

I remember that as a teenager it was my duty twice a week after school to tend our garden. During spring and summer this involved weeding the flower beds. It seemed that, no matter how often I removed those weeds, they just kept reappearing and often I was tempted to do the task less often.

However, if weeds in the garden are not removed when they first appear, they are given longer to sink their roots into the earth, and it is much more difficult to get rid of them. In the same way, arguments (even little ones) that are allowed to continue, or are merely masked by silence, get their roots deeper and deeper into the 'soil' of a relationship; they become more difficult to resolve and eventually have the potential to choke the growth of love between a husband and wife. If the problems are not dealt with effectively, they simply get worse; indeed, as new problems arise, problem is heaped upon problem, and as these 'little things' grow in number a couple may simply become weary of unresolved tensions. The 'flower bed' becomes overgrown with weeds and love can slowly die. The apostle said, 'Do not let the sun go down on your anger.' Stamp out the small problems as they arise and allow love to grow. This may involve communicating your concerns or hurts, and asking for and receiving forgiveness. It will involve being patient with each other and praying together for God's strength and wisdom in your marriage.

RESPECT EACH OTHER

The second reciprocal responsibility for husband and wife is to respect each other. In Ephesians 5:33 we read, 'Let the wife see to it that she respect her husband.' For the other side of this coin, in 1 Peter 3:7 we read, 'You husbands likewise, live with your wives in an understanding way, as with a weaker vessel, since she is a woman; and grant her honor as a fellow heir of the grace of life, so that your prayers may not be hindered.'

I want to draw your attention to two words that are used in these passages. In Ephesians 5:33, wives are told to 'respect' their husbands. In the original Greek, the word used is *phobetai*[11] from *phobeo*,[12] meaning 'to fear'. In its context it means reverential fear or respect. In 1 Peter 3:7 the Greek word used is *timen*,[13] meaning 'honour'. This word *timen* is used in Matthew 27:9 to mean 'valuing Christ at a price'. In the *Oxford English Dictionary* the primary meaning of 'honour' is 'to give high respect'. Therefore, wives are to respect their husbands, and husbands are to have a high respect, or a special respect, for their wives! I think that is absolutely wonderful! Only God in his infinite wisdom could think of such a thing: that a high respect, or a special respect, should be given to the weaker vessel.

Look again at 1 Peter 3:7: 'You husbands likewise, live with your wives in an understanding way, as with a weaker vessel, since she is a woman; and grant her honor ...' In man's economy it is the strong who demand respect; in God's economy it is the weak who deserve high respect, a respect that is enveloped in loving care and compassion.

Of course, respect, even though it is a duty and therefore must be performed, is made much easier if it is earned. I'm sure you will agree with me when I say that it is difficult to respect someone who does not deserve it. It is difficult to respect someone who says and does things that are unseemly or even hurtful. Therefore, it is extremely important that a husband and wife behave towards each other in a manner that deserves respect. On this point, John Angell James says, 'Moral esteem is one of the firmest supports and strongest guards of love ... and a high degree of excellence cannot fail to produce such esteem.'[14]

Simply put, this means that your conduct towards your partner should, as much as possible, be the best possible. Now, that's no easy task. In the marriage relationship a couple will (or should) get to know each other better than they know anyone else, and in the privacy of the home and the intimacy of married life, the most negative aspects of a person's character cannot remain hidden. Shortcomings will appear, and every piece of sinful conduct has the potential to damage a couple's esteem for each other. Therefore, a couple should make every effort to win each other's respect with conduct of the highest moral excellence.

Partners can help each other develop mutual respect. On the one hand, be honest with your partner about the sin you see in his or her behaviour. It is essential that this be done in the attitude of genuine love and concern for your partner, and not simply for point-scoring. We all need to be aware of the pharisaic tendency within us to see the speck in the eyes of others while missing completely the plank in our own (Matthew 7:1–6)! Rather, gently tell your partner of his or her sins and defects, and draw them to an ever-improving Christian lifestyle by the power of a holy example.[15] Warn in times of temptation and comfort in times of struggle, and in every way help him or her in the Christian walk.

Such behaviour and practical expression of love for your partner will be a wonderful aid to building mutual respect.

Chapter 5

We find the basis for our third reciprocal responsibility in Proverbs 27:8, where we read, 'Like a bird that wanders from her nest, so is a man who wanders from his home.'

Putting together what is written in Genesis 2:24 ('A man shall leave his father and his mother, and shall cleave to his wife') with this verse from Proverbs, I think it fair to say that a married couple are intended to be companions who walk together, talk together and spend quality time together.

First of all a word to husbands and potential husbands. Sadly, there are too many men who seem fonder of spending time in any place other than in the company of their wives. This can be clearly seen in how they spend their free time. For example, I have noticed in Albania that many married men spend more time in the local café drinking coffee with friends than they do with their wives. When God said, 'It is not good for the man to be alone', I think it is fair to assume that this also means that it is not good for man's helper to be alone! I believe that many men are failing in their God-given responsibility as husbands and fathers if they are more often 'out with the boys' than at home with the wives and families that God has given them. Can a man fulfil his responsibilities to his wife and family if he is rarely at home? Can he help his wife to manage their home? Can he instruct his family in the Word of God, and be a godly example to them, if he is rarely there during waking hours? Remember, woman was given to help man, not to be his slave.

God's Word says, 'Like a bird that wanders from her nest, so is a man who wanders from his home.' Commenting on this verse, Matthew Henry pointed out three important things. Firstly, it describes folly. Such men are like a silly bird that hops from branch to branch but rests nowhere. Secondly, this behaviour is unsafe. The bird that wanders is exposed to dangers, just as men are exposed to temptations, and become easy prey. Thirdly, it is neglectful. Just as the eggs and young birds are neglected and exposed to danger without the watchful eye of the parent bird, so is the family of the man who wanders from his home. In summary, Matthew Henry said, 'Those that love to wander … leave their work at home undone.' It is imperative that a married man spends sufficient time at home with his wife and family.

Furthermore, it is important that a married man spends *quality* time at home. It is not enough just to be under the same roof with your wife and family. How you spend your time with them is of the utmost importance. Let me give you a few examples from observations that I have made.

- 'Overtime' at home. How often it happens that a man comes home from work at the appropriate time, let's say 5–5.30 pm, but bringing a heap of work home with him! So, instead of spending time with his family when he is at home, he spends his time doing extra work. If he is not busying himself with some paperwork, then he may be found gazing at a computer screen for hours on end.
- Television, especially sports. When that all-important football match is on TV, in how many homes do we find a wife about to have a nervous breakdown surrounded by screaming children, while the husband sits there glued to the TV screen?
- Surfing the Internet. Could this be man's latest greatest weakness? Hours on end spent in suspended animation before the computer, all in the interests of research, of course!

It is not enough simply to be in the house together. Due attention and quality time must be given to the wife and children placed under your care. This could involve a special 'family night' once a week: a night set aside so that all members of the family can spend quality time together, perhaps going out together for a walk or games in the park. It could entail a night in, playing games, story-telling or watching a video together with special snacks. Whatever form it might take, it is important to have a regular special time together as a family. Children grow up all too quickly, and before you know it they are off doing their own thing with their friends. Make the most of the time you have with them now.

Allow me now to address wives. Remember what we read in Titus 2:3–5:

Older women likewise are to be reverent in their behavior, not malicious gossips, nor enslaved to much wine, teaching what is good, that they may encourage the young women to love their husbands, to love their children, to be sensible, pure, workers at home, kind, being subject to their own husbands, that the word of God may not be dishonored.

From all of the things said here to young wives I want to draw your attention to just one that relates directly to the point in hand. Young wives should be 'workers at home' (v. 5). Here I am on dangerous territory; I have just stepped into a minefield! Why? Is it because the Word of God is not clear? No! It is very clear. Is it because I'm about to say something contrary to the Word of God? No! I am simply going to let the Word of God speak for itself. I am in dangerous territory because feminist thinking has infiltrated the church and has distorted the Word of God beyond recognition. As God's children we must be faithful to God's Word, and we are not being faithful to God's Word if we accept only those parts which best please us. God says that young wives are to be 'workers at home'. This is very clear. The implication is that wives must spend quality time at home. In fact, I would go so far as to say that their priority should be that of homemakers and not wage-earners.

There are many expositors of God's Word in our day who believe that such an understanding of this passage is due more to 19th-century middle class ideology than to biblical exegesis. I'm not so sure that we can dismiss this passage so easily. Certainly it is clear that Paul does not tell women to remain 'cloistered at home'.[16] In fact, the passage before us shows that women are to exercise their gifts, especially in the discipleship of younger women. Proverbs 31:10–31 in particular makes it very clear that a woman may have other work and that she can in fact be a very industrious person both inside and outside the home. Nevertheless, probably the most significant roles that God has given to women are those of wife and mothers and, more generally, of homemaker.

Much of Proverbs 31:10–31 deals with the role of the virtuous wife in the home, and is interesting not only for what it says but also for what it does not say.[17] 'There is no mention of rights or pursuit of self-serving interests; neither is the husband assigned to the domestic pursuits.'[18] Keeping the home is God's assignment for the wife and mother.[19]

We must not come to the false conclusion that the Bible is against the idea of women having a role or career outside the four walls of the home. The New Testament and Proverbs make it clear that they may. However, neither must we come to the conclusion that the home can be neglected in favour of career choices. Whatever role or career a wife may be involved in outside the home must not hinder her role as wife, mother and homemaker. 'We must realize that the emphasis on the home is the very point of the Proverbs passage. Here, then, are the keys to the question of a wife and mother working outside the home: Is it beneficial to her family, does it aid her husband in his calling, and does it, in correlation with these first two, bring good to others?'[20]

Both the husband, as the main provider for the family,[21] and the wife, as provider and homemaker, are duty bound to spend quality time at home. Wives, if your work or career is taking you away from your primary responsibilities as wife and mother, then perhaps you need to sit down before God with an open Bible and an open heart, and ask God to help you regulate your life. Husbands, the world's idea of a 'man' and God's idea of a 'man' are opposed to each other. The world's idea is of a macho man who shuns his responsibilities in the home in favour of spending time with his friends. God's idea is of one who fulfils his God-given responsibilities to his family, who is not afraid to get his hands dirty changing a child's nappy, nor to get his hands clean helping with the dishes. This does not mean a husband, or, for that matter, a wife, may not go out for the evening with friends. It simply means that common sense must prevail and responsibilities must be fulfilled if a family is to function well and as God intended.

BE PATIENT WITH EACH OTHER

The need for patience is one we find as a general principle to be applied by all. In 1 Corinthians 13 Paul writes extensively on the theme of love, and amid the characteristics he uses to describe it he says, 'love is patient'. In Ephesians 4:1–3 we also read, 'I, therefore, the prisoner of the Lord, entreat you to walk in a manner worthy of the calling with which you have been called, with all humility and gentleness, with patience, showing forbearance to one another in love, being diligent to preserve the unity of the Spirit in the bond of peace.'

From the context of both passages it is clear that this is a principle and a duty that we owe to everyone, primarily our brothers and sisters in the Lord but also to our enemies. If this is so, then how much more should a man or woman express patience towards the closest friend that God has given him or her? Yet in many marriages the lack of patience is obvious. So often a husband will have had the worst possible day at work and will have managed to remain calm in the midst of the difficulties—that is, until he gets home. Then, perhaps because the supper is not ready on time, or for whatever reason something goes wrong, what happens? All the frustrations of the day are poured out in a burst of anger against his wife or children, and even the dog may receive a kick! At such times it is well to remember that love is patient. Leave the frustrations of work in the place of work, and exercise godly patience with your family.

It would be rather naïve to suggest, or even leave the impression, that no frustrations will arise in the home itself. Of course they will. It is part of our fallen nature that husbands will sometimes do things that irritate their wives, and wives will sometimes do things that irritate their husbands. As I pointed out in Chapter 3, young couples should enter marriage remembering that they are not getting married to an angel. A friend of mine once related to me the story of a man who told his friend that he was married to an angel; his friend replied, 'You're lucky. My wife's still alive!' The reality is that each marriage is the union of one sinful child of Adam with another sinful child of Adam. With that reality firmly fixed in your mind, you will be prepared to meet and accept some imperfections in your partner's behaviour, and accept that you also are imperfect and will make mistakes. Think of it this way: because you are not perfect and you make mistakes, your partner will need to be patient with you! Therefore you should also be patient with your partner. 'Love is patient.'

Patience may often appear as something passive, but it need not be so. Think of the hard-working husband who arrives home from work to find the dinner is not ready and so, trying to be patient, picks up the daily newspaper and begins to read it, all the time waiting patiently for his wife to meet his needs. In the meantime, his wife is left to get on with the task of bathing the children before tucking them safely into bed for the night, at which point she can then focus upon dinner. In such cases patience ought to be active. Patience also involves helping the busy wife, either by helping with the children or by rolling up your sleeves and beginning to prepare dinner. Husbands, remember: you may have had a busy day at work, but your wife has probably had a busy day also. The same applies to working wives, of course, and the principle is even more appropriate in homes where both partners work in salaried employment.

'Patience', however, does not mean 'blind acceptance'. What do I mean by that? To make mountains out of molehills or to be constantly nagging or finding faults in your partner, especially over small matters, is certainly a danger to be avoided.[22] However, refusing to be honest with yourself or your partner is equally dangerous, especially if the issues involved are important. In Proverbs 27:6 we read, 'Faithful are the wounds of a friend …' John Angell James puts it like this: Love '… does not forbid … but actually demands that we should… mutually point out our faults.'[23]

As mentioned earlier, this should be done carefully, and certainly not spitefully. To take the apostle Paul's words on the subject, we should 'speak the truth in love' (Ephesians 4:15). Christian counsellors and pastors are often faced with situations where couples have hidden, denied, excused or justified difficulties and faults for years.[24] For a long period of time they have hidden the truth about how they feel. They say things like, 'It's just a little thing …'; ' It doesn't really bother me …'; 'His bark is worse than his bite …', etc. But finally they reach their limit, and cannot take it any longer. Then, out of frustration, hurt or despair, they explode. God's way is to deal with the 'little foxes' (Song of Solomon 2:15) as they appear. Speak the truth in love, and help your partner to deal constructively and wisely with his or her faults.

At this point I must qualify what I have just said with a small word of advice. Couples should never point out each other's faults in anger; neither should they ever point out a partner's faults in public, even if those faults arise in public. Love is patient, and, as the preacher said in Ecclesiastes 3:7, there is a time to be silent and a time to speak. Wait until you are alone in the privacy of your own home and then talk openly about such things. Remember that the reason for pointing each other's faults is to ensure that pardon is sought and forgiveness given. It should never be a case of seeking revenge or settling scores (Leviticus 19:18). It is also important to learn to forgive your partner quickly for those issues that you find difficult to ignore. Don't make the mistake of thinking you can simply put a matter behind you if in reality it continues to upset you. Deal with every issue openly and honestly with your partner. Be patient in trying to find out why your partner behaved in a certain way. Talk with each other and try at least to understand your partner's point of view, even if you don't agree with it. This all helps in developing a patient response that should, in turn, lead to a clearer understanding and the ability to put the issue behind, or, if necessary, for forgiveness to be sought and given before a small problem has time to escalate into something bigger.

Furthermore, exercise wisdom in choosing the faults you do talk about. Not every small shortcoming needs to be pointed out all the time. Proverbs 19:11 tells us that 'A man's discretion makes him slow to anger, and it his glory to overlook a transgression.' There will be many occasions, especially in marriage, when it is wise to overlook an offence. Indeed, this is true of life in general. How many arguments could be rendered unnecessary and how many hurts be avoided if only God's children would occasionally overlook small offences! Be patient with each other. Learn to overlook small faults.

BEAR EACH OTHER'S BURDENS

Our final reciprocal responsibility for husbands and wives is found in Galatians 6:2, where the apostle Paul writes, 'Bear one another's burdens, and thus fulfill the law of Christ.' This may be taken as referring specifically to the verse immediately before, that is, that we should be sympathetic towards those overtaken by sin, recognizing that we could also fall. More generally, it may be seen as an exhortation simply to be more aware of one another's needs and particular burdens, and to be ever willing to help our brothers and sisters when we see them in need.[25]

Applied more specifically to husbands and wives, there are numerous practical applications for this principle. For example, husbands and wives should feel that they can talk freely with each other about all their fears and concerns. Many husbands, wanting to protect their wives from unnecessary worry, keep problems hidden from them. However, women, particularly wives, are very discerning. They know when something is not well. So, husbands, don't try to hide your fears from your wife. Remember that your wife is the closest friend and helper that God has given you. Talk with her; seek her counsel and her comfort. As for wives, knowing that men are often prone to keep problems bottled up inside, encourage your husband to talk freely with you about his concerns and fears. As John

Angell James puts it, 'If she cannot counsel, then she can comfort ... If she cannot relieve his cares, she can help bear them ... If she cannot offer wisdom, she can spread the matter before God, the fountain of wisdom.'[26]

In a similar manner, husbands should listen to their wife's concerns. How many young wives and mothers, having worked hard all day, need someone to listen to them? That's all: they simply need someone who will listen. Very often wives want someone to pay close attention to them as they talk about the events or difficulties of the day. In his book *Men are from Mars, Women are from Venus*, John Gray says this: 'Many times a woman just wants to share her feelings about her day, and her husband ... thinking he is helping ... interrupts her by offering a steady flow of solutions to her problems.'[27] The point that John Gray is making is that a man very often makes the mistake of trying to change how his wife feels by offering solutions to her problems, when in actual fact all she really wants is for her husband to listen. Whatever you may think of John Gray's observations, James tells us in James 1:19, 'But let everyone be quick to hear [and] slow to speak ...' Bear your partner's burdens simply by listening attentively to what he or she has to say, and then lay the matter before God in prayer.

Much more could be said on this matter of reciprocal responsibilities between husbands and wives. That both partners have duties to perform and responsibilities to fulfil towards each other is very clear from the Scriptures. However, the interesting thing is that the duties and responsibilities God sets out in the Bible are not burdensome. In fact, they ought to be a pleasure, and actually help us to build marriages that are strong, beautiful and full of love. Who could ask for more?

Study questions

FOR DISCUSSION

1. What do you understand by 'joint responsibilities'?
2. Read 1 Corinthians 13:1–8.
   (a) Make a list of the various attributes of love mentioned in this passage.
   (b) Discuss the practical applications of each attribute within the context of marriage.
3. Read Ephesians 5:33 and 1 Peter 3:7.

Chapter 5

   (a) What do these passages teach us about mutual respect in the context of marriage?

   (b) Make a short list of ways in which husbands and wives can seek to earn each other's respect.

4. Discuss Matthew Henry's comment: 'those that love to wander … leave their work at home undone.'

5. What do you consider to be 'quality time'?

6. Read 1 Corinthians 13:4.

   (a) In what practical ways can we show our partners that 'love is patient'?

   (b) What is the main difference between 'patience' and 'blind acceptance'?

7. Read Galatians 6:2.

   (a) Make a list of practical applications from this verse.

   (b) Discuss the list.

FOR PERSONAL REFLECTION

8. Reflect upon the following:

   (a) 'Marriage is more about responsibilities than rights.'

   (b) How does your thinking on responsibilities in marriage measure up to the biblical standard?

   (c) In what ways can you seek to win your partner's respect?

Notes

1 Quotation from http://theologica.blogspot.com/2005_02_01_archive.html

2 Many of the ideas contained in this chapter are found in an excellent study on the subject in Chapter 2 of **John Angell James,** *A Help to Domestic Happiness*.

3 ἀγάπη. Both **Fritz Rienecker** (*Linguistic Key to the New Testament* (Grand Rapids: Zondervan, 1976), p. 431) and **Gordon D. Fee** (*The First Epistle to the Corinthians*, NICNT (Grand Rapids: Eerdmans, 1987)) recommend the following book for further reading on this word: James Moffatt, *Love in the New Testament* (New York, 1930).

4 φίλανδρος,—loving one's husband.

5 Sometimes both *agape* and *phileo* are used to express love towards the same object, but 'the distinction between the two verbs remains, and they are never used indiscriminately in the same passage; if each word is used with reference to the same objects, each word

retains its distinctive and essential character' (**W. E. Vine,** *Vine's Expository Dictionary of New Testament Words* (Peabody: Hendrickson, n. d.), p. 703).

6 אַהֲבָה; See **William L. Holladay** (ed.), *A Concise Hebrew and Aramaic Lexicon of the Old Testament* (Grand Rapids: Eerdmans, 1988), p. 5.

7 For a fuller definition of 'love' see **R. Mohrlang's** definition in *A Dictionary of Paul and His Letters* (Leicester: IVP, 1993), p. 577; and **F. H. Palmer's** definition in *The New Bible Dictionary* (London: IVP, 1962), p. 752.

8 Gordon D. Fee, *The First Epistle to the Corinthians*, NICNT (Eerdmans, 1987), p. 279.

9 By 'ordinary cases' I refer to healthy couples for whom all aspects of love are possible. For situations where circumstances dictate that certain aspects of love may not be fulfilled, perhaps due to illness or accident, I believe that God gives grace in keeping with the need (see 2 Corinthians 12:9).

10 As Christians we are also duty-bound to love even our enemies (Matthew 5:44), but that is outside the scope of this study.

11 Φοβῆται.

12 φοβέω. See **Thayer's** *Greek-English Lexicon of the New Testament* (Grand Rapids: Baker, 1977), p. 655.

13 τιμήν Ibid. p. 624.

14 James, *A Help to Domestic Happiness*, p. 17.

15 Ibid. p. 29.

16 S. M. Baugh, 'A foreign world: Ephesians in the first century', in *Women in the Church: A Fresh Analysis of 1 Timothy 2:9–15*, **Köstenberger, Schreiner and Baldwin** (eds) (Grand Rapids: Baker Book House, 1995), pp. 49–50.

17 Arguments from 'silence' should never be used to build doctrines. Nevertheless, they are useful for the purpose of clarification.

18 Dorothy Patterson, 'The high calling of wife and mother in biblical perspective', in *Recovering Biblical Manhood and Womanhood*, p. 367.

19 Ibid.

20 George W. Knight III, 'The family and the church: How should biblical manhood and womanhood work out in practice?', Ibid. p. 348.

21 In 1 Timothy 5:8 the one rebuked for not providing is male, e.g., 'his household' and 'his own'.

22 James, p. 25.

23 Ibid.

24 Mack, *Your Family God's Way*, p. 144.

25 This verse '… directs us to sympathize with one another under the various trials and troubles that we may meet with, and be ready to afford each other the comfort and counsel, the help and assistance, which our circumstances may require' (Matthew Henry, *Commentary on the Whole Bible* (Macdonald Publishing Company, n. d.), vol. 6, p. 679).

26 James, p. 26, with slight modifications to the language used.

27 John Gray, *Men are from Mars, Women are from Venus* (Thorsons, 1992), p. 22.

A special duty for wives

Be subject to one another in the fear of Christ. Wives, be subject to your own husbands, as to the Lord. For the husband is the head of the wife, as Christ also is the head of the church, He Himself being the Savior of the body (Ephesians 5:21–23).

Just who is the boss?

One night, the pastor of a local church had a row with his wife. His neighbour listened with interest, and his curiosity was particularly aroused when the row came to an end after a dreadful clamour on the stairs. The next morning the neighbour met the pastor in the street and asked, 'What was all that noise last night?'

'Nothing much,' replied the pastor, 'just my wife throwing my clothes down the stairs.'

'What!' exclaimed the neighbour. 'Your clothes made all that noise?'

'Well, yes,' said the pastor. 'Mind you, I was still inside them!'

Another story is told of a pastor who, during a church outing, was seen to give in or submit to the pleas of his wife on a number of occasions. One church member was delighted with the opportunity to challenge his pastor, and asked why he hadn't put into practice what he had preached on the subject of headship in the home.

'I thought you were the head of your family,' said the neighbour.

'I am,' replied the pastor swiftly, 'but my wife is the neck that turns me.'

To some extent the stories above highlight the fact that marriage is often seen as a conflict of wills. On the one hand, there is the influence of the emancipation movement, which says that wives must insist upon their rights as equals. On the other hand, there still remain strongholds of male chauvinism, with many husbands determined to 'keep the wife in her place'. By now, in light of previous chapters, it should not come as a surprise to hear that both these extremes are contrary to God's ideal for marriage. God intended marriage to be a place of peace rather than a war zone, a place of harmony not controversy, and it is often the failure to put into practice God-given principles of leadership in the home that has led to so much domestic turmoil.

With that in mind, I think it is fair to say that in these studies we have reached perhaps the most controversial part. Having looked at all the key passages in the Bible on this subject and having read a number of reliable authors, I believe it is clear that the Bible teaches just one fundamental duty of wives. Upon this one duty all the other duties of wives are built. Interestingly, mention of the duty in question is found in no fewer than four verses of Scripture (Ephesians 5:21; 5:22; Colossians 3:18; 1 Peter 3:1), and in each of these verses the same Greek word is used. That word is *hupotasso*[1] meaning 'submit', and the special duty expected of wives is 'be subject [or submit] to your own husbands, as to the Lord'.

For many women, living as they do at the beginning of the 21st century, the whole idea of submission to male leadership is offensive. Besides, many will argue, Ephesians 5:21 makes it very clear that submission is a responsibility for all believers. That is indeed true. From the context of the verse we see that the truly Spirit-filled person will display the meekness and gentleness of Christ. One of the clearest characteristics of that Spirit-filled life is submission to one another. Nevertheless, this does not negate the fact that on three other occasions the Scriptures address wives specifically, enjoining them to submit to their husbands:

- 'Wives, be subject to your own husbands, as to the Lord' (Ephesians 5:22).
- 'Wives, be subject to your husbands, as is fitting in the Lord' (Colossians 3:18).
- 'Wives, be submissive to your own husbands' (1 Peter 3:1).

This is indeed a controversial area, but it is my sincere conviction that it is controversial simply because many men and women have wrong ideas, misconceptions and preconceptions, about what biblical submission actually involves. Therefore, right at the beginning I am going to take the controversy out of this theme by outlining exactly what I intend to say. Firstly, I would like to clear up some misunderstandings by explaining what biblical submission is not. Only then will we consider what biblical submission actually is. In doing so we will look briefly at the Greek verbs used in the Bible and follow that by taking a couple of examples of submission from the life of Christ. Finally, we will look at God's reason for such submission.

What submission is not

Perhaps one of the commonest misconceptions about biblical submission is that it implies that a wife is inferior to her husband. A proper understanding of submission in the biblical context shows this to be an unfounded notion in the husband–wife relationship. Perhaps you will remember that in Chapter 2 we looked at Genesis 2:18, where God says, 'I will make him a helper suitable for him.' We looked at the Hebrew words used there—*ezer kenegdo*—and saw how the word *ezer* (meaning 'help') is used elsewhere in Scripture to describe God as a 'helper' of his people. Obviously, if God is to be God, this cannot mean that he is inferior to his people. Therefore, when the woman was described in Genesis 2:18 as man's helper, this did not mean that she was inferior to Adam or that she was his slave.

We also saw that the word *kenegdo* literally means 'according to what is in front of him', a term which implies equality. Let me remind you of those beautiful words of Matthew Henry on this verse: 'The woman was made of a rib out of the side of Adam; not made out of his head to rule over him, nor out of his feet to be trampled upon by him, but out of his side to be equal with him, under his arm to be protected, and near to his heart to be loved.'

The point is that even from Genesis we know that God intended husband and wife to be 100 per cent equal. Therefore, whatever it does mean for a wife to submit to her husband, it does not mean that she is his inferior. Furthermore, as I have already mentioned, several passages teach that we are *all* to submit to one another; clearly we cannot all be inferior to one another.

The life of Christ illustrates beautifully that biblical submission does not imply inferiority. In Luke 2:51 we read, 'And He went down with them [Mary and Joseph] … and He continued in subjection [submission] to them.'

Here we have Jesus, the Son of God, God in human flesh, submitting to his human parents (the very same Greek word that is used for the submission of wives to their husbands is used here). Now it is very obvious that Jesus was in no way inferior to his human parents, yet he submitted to them. In the same way, the submission of wives in no way implies that they are inferior to their husbands.

Secondly, submission does not mean that a wife cannot have work outside her domestic duties in the home. In other words, the Bible does not teach that wives cannot have wage-earning jobs. In Proverbs 31:10–16 we read:

An excellent wife, who can find?
For her worth is far above jewels …
She looks for wool and flax,
And works with her hands in delight.
She is like merchant ships;
She brings her food from afar.
She rises also while it is still night …
She considers a field and buys it;
From her earnings she plants a vineyard.

The very least that can be said about this passage is that it shows how a wife can be a very industrious person. I believe that verse 16 in particular ('She considers a field and buys it …') teaches that such industry may extend beyond the four walls of the home, and that a wife may indeed have a career.

Thirdly, submission does not mean that a wife cannot offer her husband advice, or that she must accept without any discussion everything her husband says. Look again at Proverbs 31:26, where the writer clearly states, 'She opens her mouth in wisdom …'

Now if the Word of God says that the godly wife 'opens her mouth in wisdom', surely it is a foolish man indeed who does not listen to the wise advice that she offers. In 1 Samuel 25 we read the story of Nabal and Abigail. David, who had protected Nabal's workers for some time, had sent some of his men to Nabal to ask for food. However, Nabal rebuked them and sent them away with nothing. At this point Abigail intervened, realizing that her husband's actions could have very serious consequences. She set out quickly to meet David, taking with her 200 loaves of bread, 5 sheep and many other items of food. When she finally caught up with David, she pleaded with him not to cause unnecessary bloodshed. David's reply is significant: 'Blessed be your discernment, and blessed be you, who have kept me this day from bloodshed' (1 Samuel 25:32–33). As a result, David, who had intended to punish Nabal and his household, did not kill anyone, and God himself dealt with Nabal.

Don't you think that Nabal could have spared everyone a lot of trouble if he had only sought the wise counsel of his wife Abigail? In the same way, any husband would do well to seek the advice of the helper that God has given him.

The nature of submission

Having considered what submission is not, let's now consider what the Bible says submission actually is. Firstly, let's consider the Greek words used. As we have seen, in four verses that refer directly to wives (Ephesians 5:21–22; Colossians 3:18; and 1 Peter 3:1), the word used is taken from the verb *hupotasso*. This word is actually made up of two Greek words: *hupo*, meaning 'under', and *tasso* meaning 'to arrange in an orderly manner'. Put together it simply means 'to put under an orderly arrangement', 'to be a particular order', or 'to submit oneself to a particular order'. In these four verses, it means that wives are to be under, or are to submit to, the order that God has ordained. That is, wives are to submit to their husbands because God has ordained that the husband be the head of the wife.

The second thing we learn from the Greek verb is that this is a command. In Colossians 3:18, the form used is the present imperative. Therefore, it is imperative that wives submit. It is not an optional extra. It is not something that wives can accept or reject according to their circumstances. If wives are to please God and live according to God's order, they must submit to their husbands.

The third thing we learn from the Greek verb is that this is to be a continuous action. In every verse the verb is in the present tense, and this signifies that the wife's submission is to be continuous or ongoing. It is not something to be done in the past, nor is it something to be done sometime in the future. Rather, submission is something that wives should be doing now and doing it continually in their homes.

So much for the verbs used. Now let's look at a word Paul uses in Ephesians 5:24. 'But as the church is subject to Christ, so also the wives ought to be [subject] to their husbands in everything.' The word that I want to draw your attention to is found at the very end of this verse: the Greek word used is *panti*, which simply means 'all things'. What is the significance of this word? Well, it simply means that a wife's submission should be comprehensive. The wife should not simply submit to her husband in the things in which she believes him to be correct.

Imagine for a moment that a very important decision must be made in the home. The husband, recognizing his wife's godly discernment, discusses the matter thoroughly with her. Perhaps the discussion continues for several weeks, but in the end the husband is not convinced that his wife's point of view is correct, and the wife is not convinced that her husband's point of view is correct. How is such a situation resolved? Well, the husband, as head of the family and the one whom God will hold accountable, must make the final decision. This decision can be based solely on his own opinion, or solely on his wife's opinion, or a combination of the two. The point is that *the husband* must make the decision, and the wife must submit to that decision. The only times when a wife should not submit to her husband's decisions are (a) when they would cause her (or others) to do something that God forbids, or (b) when they would cause her (or others) not to do something that God commands.[2] In such cases, a wife ought to follow the principle found in Acts 5:28–29. On that occasion Peter and the other apostles were forbidden to preach the word of God openly, but their response was, 'we must obey God rather than men.' Therefore, on occasions when obedience to a husband's decision would entail disobeying God, the wife must obey God rather than her husband.

Having considered what the original Greek teaches us about the nature of biblical submission, let us now look at a couple of examples from the life of Christ. In Philippians 2:5–8 we read:

Have this attitude in yourselves which was also in Christ Jesus, who, although He existed in the form of God, did not regard equality with God a thing to be grasped, but emptied Himself, taking the form of a bond-servant, and being made in the likeness of men. And being found in appearance as a man, He humbled Himself by becoming obedient to the point of death, even death on a cross.

This passage teaches us that, although Christ was 100 per cent equal with God, yet he humbled himself and gave up his equal standing with God. It is important at this point to stress that this did not entail Christ changing in his equal essence or nature; such a change would have made him less than God. What Christ gave up was his equal position with God in eternity, or, as Louis Berkhof puts it, 'his being on an equality with God'.[3] In other words, he left his sinless throne in heaven and entered a sin-cursed world, and there submitted to the will of God the Father. In this sense he gave up his independent exercise of authority, and submitted to the authority of the Father.[4]

This was a voluntary action. Christ voluntarily gave up his authority. In the same way, a wife's submission is to be a voluntary act. It is something the wife should do willingly, not grudgingly.

In John 4:34 we read Christ's words describing his mission on earth: 'My food is to do the will of Him who sent me.' From this we find that not only did Christ voluntarily submit to the Father, but also that his submission was a source of strength: it was his 'food'. Marriage has been described as the only war where you sleep in the same bed as your enemy. However, when we have a correct understanding of what biblical submission is, we see that, rather than it being something that causes strife or tension between the sexes, it actually nourishes and strengthens, feeding the husband–wife relationship. By its very nature biblical submission removes tension and makes a family stronger. God's recipe for a healthy family—*God's* recipe, remember—cannot fail. God knows what is best for us. Do you believe that? If so, 'wives, be subject to your husbands'.

Finally, let's look briefly at some biblical reasons for wives submitting to their husbands.

Biblical reasons for submission

Firstly, it is a spiritual duty. In Colossians 3:18 we read, 'Wives, be subject to your husbands, as is fitting in the Lord', and Ephesians 5:22 says, 'Wives, be subject to your own husbands, as to the Lord'. At this point I want to draw your attention to two phrases in these verses: firstly, 'as is fitting in the Lord', and secondly, 'as to the Lord'.

B. M. Palmer beautifully and succinctly captures the essence of these phrases when he says that they lift the wife's submission to a higher level of consecration and service to Almighty God.[5] Ephesians 5:24 elaborates on this point: 'As the church is subject to Christ, so also the wives ought to be to their husbands'. Now, let me ask you this: When the Bible exhorts us to pray without ceasing, do we question the need to pray? Or when the Bible exhorts us, as Christians, to obey the commands of Christ and to live moral lives, do we question the need to live as God desires? Of course not. Due to our still-imperfect natures and the remnants of sin in every believer, we will sometimes fail in these areas. We may sometimes forget to pray, or we may occasionally disobey the commands of Christ, or we may fail to live as we ought. Nevertheless, we would never question that as Christians we should obey Christ in all things. In the whole area of submission, wives have a religious obligation to submit to their husbands. They are to submit as to the Lord. Their submission is not to a 'superior male'; rather, in submitting to their husbands they are in fact submitting to the rule of their God and Saviour who has placed the husband in the position of accountability.

Herein lies the wonderful thing: how can there be any sense of inferiority, or degradation, in the wife submitting to her husband when this submission is in fact a submission to the authority of God? If only people—husbands and wives—could realize the true nature of biblical submission, and the biblical reason for submission, I believe that submission would become a delight as it is offered in service to an almighty and wonderful God.

This leads us to a second reason for submission: that there is need for order and accountability. In 1 Corinthians 11:3 we read, 'But I want you to understand that Christ is the head of every man, and the man is the head of a woman, and God is the head of Christ.'

There is a very clear order here. God is the head of Christ, Christ is the head of man, and man is the head of woman. Take special notice of the fact that there is not only order in the family, there is also order within the Godhead. Again, this does not teach that Christ was inferior to the Father. Rather, it simply teaches that there is a very definite structure for the division of work and responsibility. In the same way, God has ordained a definite structure for the division of work and responsibility in the home.

The husband, as head of the home, is accountable to God for the condition of his family. Remember when Eve took the fruit of the tree in

Eden, and sin entered the world (Genesis 3)? Who did God hold accountable for this action? It was Adam! This is made very clear in Romans 5. That whole chapter teaches us that sin entered the world through Adam. Even though it was Eve who sinned first, Adam was held accountable. Why? Simply because he was head of the family unit.

One young lady, on hearing this teaching, turned to her boyfriend and said, 'This is wonderful news for women.'

'Oh,' he said, 'why?'

'Well,' she said, 'when we get married I can sin all I want and you will get the blame!'

Scripture does not allow us to take it this far, but the principle is clear. God has decreed a structure and an order of accountability within the family.

Wives, God has given you one special duty. Are you prepared to fulfil this duty with joyful hearts, knowing that, in doing so, you are serving God as he intended you to serve him, and trusting God that he knows what is best for you and for your family?

Of course, it is worth pointing out that submission is made easier for a wife whenever her husband loves her as Christ loves the church (Ephesians 5:25). It is to this that we shall direct our attention in the next chapter.

Study questions

FOR DISCUSSION

1. Read Genesis 2:18 and 1 Samuel 7:12. What do these passages teach us about submission within marriage?
2. Discuss Matthew Henry's comment on Genesis 2:18 (see under 'What submission is not').
3. What does Proverbs 31:26 teach us about submission in marriage?
4. What can we learn about submission from the Greek word *hupatasso*?
5. What are the practical implications of the Greek word *panti* in Ephesians 5:24?
6. Discuss this statement: 'How can there be any sense of inferiority or degradation in a wife submitting to her husband when this submission is in fact a submission to the authority of God?'

Chapter 6

7. How does your understanding of submission compare to the biblical expression of submission? In what practical ways can you demonstrate your acceptance of biblical submission to your partner?

Notes

1 ὑποτάσσομαι from ὑποτάσσω: 'To line oneself up under. Used in a military sense of soldiers submitting to their superior …' (**Rienecker** on Ephesians 5:21, *Linguistic Key to the New Testament* (Grand Rapids: Zondervan, 1976), p. 538).

2 **Mack,** *Strengthening your Marriage,* p. 15.

3 **Louis Berkhof,** *Systematic Theology* (Edinburgh: Banner of Truth, 1958), p. 328.

4 See **Hendriksen,** *New Testament Commentary: Philippians, Colossians and Philemon* (Grand Rapids: Baker Book House, 1979), p. 108.

5 **Palmer,** *The Family,* p. 70.

A special duty for husbands

Husbands, love your wives, just as Christ also loved the church and gave Himself up for her … So husbands ought also to love their own wives as their own bodies. He who loves his own wife loves himself (Ephesians 5:25,28).

Mission impossible!

Some years ago, a pastor speaking to me on the topic of leadership in the home said, 'The problem with men in the home is that they are not being men.' The point that he was making was that biblical male leadership in the home fails because too many men are weak leaders, or not leaders at all. With their husbands failing in this way, wives take on a much more domineering role in the home. Most of the major decisions that need to be made are left up to the wife, along with the necessary nurturing and even discipline of children. Another friend (not a pastor) once explained to me the following method of finding a wife (I was at that time in my late twenties and still a bachelor): he suggested that I take a club and in true caveman style club a woman on the head, and drag her by the hair back to my 'cave'.

There are two very vivid pictures of men here. Firstly, we see the weakling who willingly abdicates his responsibilities. Secondly, we see the aggressive strong man who, by his physical strength and strong personality, makes it absolutely clear who is boss in his house. At the outset of our study, I want to dismiss both these pictures as wrong views of leadership in the home.

That the husband is to be the leader in the home is very clear in Scripture. We saw this in our last study when we looked at the one special duty of wives. Let's remind ourselves of Paul's words: 'But I want you to understand that Christ is the head of every man, and the man is the head of a woman, and God is the head of Christ' (1 Corinthians 11:3); and 'For the husband is the head of the wife' (Ephesians 5:23).

So the husband is the head of the wife and he is to be the head or leader in the home. But what exactly does this mean? What does it involve? What does it mean for the husband to be the 'head' or 'leader' of his wife? I believe that biblical leadership in the home is defined by one very important word. Remember the instruction in Ephesians 5:25 that Paul gives to husbands: 'Husbands, love your wives …'

It is interesting that, when Paul commands wives to submit, he does not say, 'Wives, submit … Husbands, rule or boss your wives around.' Rather, he says, 'Wives, submit … Husbands, love.'[1] Three times in this one passage husbands are told to love their wives: we have just read it in verse 25, and we see it again in verse 28 ('So husbands ought also to love their own wives as their own bodies') and in verse 33 ('Let each individual among you also love his own wife even as himself').

You may remember that in Chapter 5 we saw that love is to be reciprocal in the home: husband and wife are to love each other. Just as Ephesians 5:21 teaches that submission is a mutual responsibility and yet is enjoined upon the wife in a special way, so love must be mutual in the home, yet it is enjoined upon the husband in a special way.[2] Here in Ephesians 5 we find that there is a significant relationship between headship and love. So closely are they related that Jay Adams, in his book *Christian Living in the Home*, puts the two together and dedicates a chapter to the theme of 'Loving leadership'. In fact, Adams goes so far as to say that 'leadership is nothing if it is not loving leadership'.[3]

At this point let me make it clear that a wife's submission ought not to be dependant upon her husband's love. Nor indeed is a husband's love for his wife to be dependant upon her willingness to submit to his leadership in the home. It is worth noting that both the injunctions in Ephesians stand, in a sense, independently: that is to say, even if a wife is failing in her duty before God to submit to the leadership that God has set in place, it does not negate the husband's responsibility to love his wife. In the same way, when a husband is falling short of his duty to love his wife and to couch all his leadership responsibilities in the atmosphere of genuine and tangible love, it does not negate the wife's responsibility to submit to that leadership. For exceptions to this read again my comments on Acts 5:28–29 in Chapter 6. However, it must also be stressed that, if leadership in the home is to be the sort of leadership that God intended, it ought to be so saturated in love that it becomes the desire of and pleasure for the rest of the family to submit to it. B. M. Palmer, the 19th-century theologian, sums up the husband's duties like this: 'It is worthy of special notice that, in all the apostolic injunctions, the great duty enforced upon him is love.'[4]

In this chapter, then, I want to challenge men—husbands and potential husbands—with their responsibility to be the type of leaders that God wants them to be; I want to challenge them to be 'loving leaders'.

Loving leadership involves avoiding wrong behaviour

Paul, writing to the Colossians says, 'Husbands, love your wives, and do not be embittered against them' (Colossians 3:19). He uses an interesting word: *pikraino*.[5] This verb has the idea of being harsh, sharp or bitter, and it refers to the friction caused by impatience and thoughtless nagging.[6] I think it is fair to say that, as a direct application of this verse, husbands should avoid any unnecessary display of authority. Husbands who needlessly demand obedience or exert their authority for no other reason than to parade their power are exercising an authority that is unbiblical and unhelpful, and are causing bitterness for their wives.[7] The man who demands that things must be done his way simply to show that he is boss causes his wife bitterness. The man who suppresses every thought or opinion that his wife offers; or runs his home as a dictator runs a country, possibly afraid that if he accepts other advice, his 'authority' will be undermined; such a man not only causes unnecessary bitterness for his wife but fails to understand the biblical concept of headship. Headship in the home equals leadership, not dictatorship. We saw in the previous chapter that headship involves the idea that a husband is accountable to God for the final decision on any matter in the home. But good leadership involves much more than this. It also involves a responsibility to recognize a wife's talents. Remember the virtuous wife of Proverbs 31. Her husband obviously recognized her talents and gave her freedom to express and expand them. In the same way, Christian husbands are not to crush their wife's talents; rather, they should utilize them, encourage them and rejoice in them. A husband is to be a good manager: such a manager knows how to keep his 'finger on the pulse'. He knows exactly what is being done or needs to be done, but he does not feel the need to do everything himself.

Bitterness is caused by unnecessary displays of authority, by crushing a wife's talents and also by unnecessary absence. As we have already touched on this, I won't dwell on it here; nevertheless, it is worth repeating briefly. Many men enjoy spending time 'with the boys', whether that be at the local pool hall, café or football ground. Now, there is nothing wrong with going to the café with friends or joining them to play the occasional game of pool, but when a married man spends more time with his friends than with his wife, it is time he examined his God-given responsibilities and got his priorities straight. The same applies to spending too much time at work or bringing work from the office to complete at home (see again my comments in Chapter 5 on spending quality time together). The point is that constant unnecessary absence from your wife (including being under the same roof but failing actually to function together) is a source of 'bitterness' to her.

Surveys carried out in the West on the issue of child abuse have shown that the most common form is not beating or physical abuse of varying sorts, but neglect. Simply neglecting a person's needs causes bitterness and hurt. Husbands who neglect their wife's physical, emotional or spiritual needs are failing in their God-given responsibility to be loving leaders.

In summary, then, loving leadership involves avoiding certain behaviour: unnecessary displays of power, crushing a wife's talents and unnecessary absence or neglect. However, loving leadership also involves promoting certain behaviour.

Loving leadership involves promoting right behaviour

In Ephesians 5 we find two basic criteria for good leadership in the home. The first I want to consider is found in two verses: 'Husbands ought also to love their own wives as their own bodies' (v. 28), and, 'Let each individual among you also love his own wife even as himself' (v. 33). Husbands are to love their wives as their own bodies.

LOVE YOUR WIFE AS YOUR OWN BODY

I think it is a fair to say that, generally, a modern man likes to give himself a lot of attention. He cares about his appearance and his comfort. He carefully protects his body and provides for all its needs. If a man is hungry, he eats; if he is thirsty, he drinks; if he is tired, he sleeps; if he sees an object flying towards him, he instinctively puts up his hand to protect himself.

I remember on one occasion, a man and his girlfriend were walking along a road after dark. Suddenly, out of the darkness the man saw a huge dog coming towards him barking ferociously with teeth bared. Instinctively, the man jumped behind his girlfriend for protection. Chivalry was obviously not his best quality, but thankfully (for the girl) the dog was on a chain. Now if he had really loved the girl, his instinct would have been to jump in front of her to protect her. Needless to say, the relationship didn't last very long. God says that husbands are to love their wives and protect their wives even as they protect themselves. A husband is to protect his wife, provide for her, care for her (at all times) and sacrifice for her in the same manner as he does for himself.

But the Word of God goes further than this. Not only is the husband to love his wife as himself; more significantly, he is to love her as Christ loved the church.

LOVE AS CHRIST LOVED THE CHURCH

Consider firstly what two theologians say on this point. The first is John Calvin: 'The apostle requires that they [husbands] cherish towards their wives no ordinary love, for to them he holds out the example of Christ.'[8] The second is Albert Barnes (a 19th-century theologian): 'This is the strongest love that has ever been evinced [seen] in the world ... The husband is in no danger of loving his wife too much.'[9]

If it seems difficult that wives should submit to their husbands, what is expected of husbands makes the wives' responsibility look easy in comparison. Why? Because Christ's loving leadership was perfect, and husbands are to emulate it:

WILLING TO DIE

The truth is that no husband can achieve this standard. However, while offering constant prayer to God for help, husbands must be willing to try. A husband must be willing to put the comfort of his wife before his own comfort, as Christ did for us. He must be willing to put the happiness of his wife before his own happiness, to provide her needs, to go before her in danger. He must be willing to give himself as Christ gave himself (Ephesians 5:25). Ultimately, a husband must be prepared to die for his wife.

While I do not advocate everything in the 1997 film *Titanic* starring
Leonardo DiCaprio and Kate Winslet, there is one scene that I believe
makes a valid point. Towards the end of the film, after the *Titanic* has
struck the iceberg and is doomed to sink to the bottom of the Atlantic, a
young Jack (DiCaprio) does everything in his power to protect his Rose
(Winslet). In one particular scene, when they are both in the freezing water,
Jack finds a wooden object floating on the surface. Knowing that it cannot
support the weight of them both, he pushes Rose onto it and stays in the
water himself with the knowledge that by staying in the water his own
death is inevitable. This is an example of the way a husband should be
willing to give his own life to protect his wife. But we have an even greater
example of personal sacrifice: 'Christ loved the church and gave Himself
for her.'

THE BIGGEST SERVANT

There are other implications. A husband should be willing to give his time,
energy, comfort, etc., for the sake of his wife, always keeping her interests in
mind. Christ had this to say about his own leadership: 'The Son of Man did
not come to be served, but to serve ...' (Matthew 20:28). In John 13 we read
how Jesus, the head of the church, took a towel in his hands, poured water
into a basin and washed his disciples' feet. Commenting on these passages,
Wayne Mack says, 'When we apply this biblical concept of leadership to
the husband, we see that being a leader means that he must be the family's
biggest servant.'[10] This is indeed a radical thought and one that, sadly, is far
from the reality in most homes.

THE BEST EXAMPLE

As a leader, Christ also spent a lot of time with his disciples, being an
example to them and instructing them. Sadly, in many homes husbands
neglect the whole area of biblical instruction. 1 Corinthians 14:35 gives a
clear indication that the husband has a responsibility to instruct his wife in
spiritual matters. Men, this means that you need to be 'men of the Word',
that is, men who read their Bibles regularly and know how to apply what
they read. If husbands are to be spiritual teachers for their wives, it is

obvious that they need to be instructing themselves first of all. And 'instruction' is nothing if it is not backed up by a godly example. On many occasions we read in the Gospels that Jesus said, 'Follow me', or, 'I have left you an example.' He did not simply tell people what they ought to do, he showed them how to do it. He not only told men to pray, he spent all night in prayer as an example. Husbands, what example are you setting your wives in your prayer lives? Single men, if you are thinking of marriage, the patterns of behaviour that you establish now will be reflected in your marriages. Do not think for a moment that once you are married all these principles of godly leadership will somehow simply fall into place. Do not think for a moment that you will automatically become a totally different person who will suddenly find these things a pleasure to do. It involves discipline and that discipline ought to start even before marriage. Ask yourself what sort of pattern you are establishing now for leading your future family in prayer.

Surely, then, biblical leadership in the home means that husbands must set a godly example. They must be an example in prayer, in holiness, in devotion to God, and in tenderness and compassion.

LOVE INVOLVES TAKING TIME TO UNDERSTAND

In days when gay and lesbian movements are constantly trying to minimize the essential differences between men and women, it is interesting that John Gray, in his book *Men are from Mars, Women are from Venus*, points out that men and women are intrinsically different in many ways. He highlights the need for partners to take the time to understand that men and women also communicate their needs differently from each other. Gray suggests that greater understanding of the complex emotional differences between men and women will result in more fulfilling relationships. I believe this to be absolutely true, not on the basis of secular psychology, but on the basis of God's Word. This is a point that was written in God's Word almost 2000 years ago.

In 1 Peter 3:7 we read these words: 'You husbands likewise, live with your wives in an understanding way, as with a weaker vessel …' The Greek of the New Testament literally says that men are to live with their wives 'according to knowledge'.[11] This means that husbands ought to take time to gain an ever-increasing and deepening knowledge of what makes their wives tick. One area where this can be seen is in relationships where the wife does not go out to work but whose full-time work is that of housewife and mother. A tired husband coming home from a long and possibly frustrating or difficult day at work needs to understand that his wife may also have had a frustrating and difficult day at home. A housewife can easily feel a sense of isolation, a sense of being cut off from social contact. This, of course, can be addressed in any number of practical ways. Nevertheless, a husband needs to understand that when he comes home tired and all he wants to do is sit quietly and read or watch the news, his wife may in fact need to talk through the events of her day. If Christ loved the church and gave himself for her, is it too much to ask that a husband actually sacrifice a little of his time and listen to his wife?

In the whole area of sexual relationships there are also important differences between husbands and wives (besides the obvious). Very often a husband will 'feel the urge' just by watching his wife undress for bed and may be rather perturbed when he discovers that she is not feeling the same way. In such an instance, what the husband has failed to understand is that women do not generally get sexually excited as quickly as men (there may, of course, be exceptions to the rule). There has been much written on this subject in recent years. Dr James Dobson, for example, suggests that a woman is more stimulated by the romantic qualities of her husband than simply by his appearance. He further suggests that the sexual relationship for husbands is more physical, whereas for women it is much more of a deep, emotional experience.[12] Therefore, if husbands want truly to develop their relationship with their wives, and to live with them in an understanding way, they will need to take such differences into consideration.

A further practical consideration is that at a certain time each month women go through physical and hormonal changes in their bodies. These changes are often reflected in emotional changes. Quite simply, a husband needs to be understanding of his wife at such times and be a support to her. The same is also true when wives go through the menopause. At this point I want to stress that I am no expert in medical matters, and neither do I want to create the impression that I am. For further insight into these and other medical issues I suggest that readers seek proper professional guidance from an experienced and respected doctor. I mention them here simply to introduce husbands to a few of the ways in which they can begin to live with their wives in a more understanding way, as the Scriptures exhort us to do.

It has often been said that the measure of a husband can be seen in the countenance of his wife's face. As a husband, ask yourself a couple of searching questions: How do I measure up to the standards that God has set before me? How is this reflected in my wife's sense of joy and happiness within our relationship? As I have already stated, no husband can ever live up to the perfect standard of Christ. Because of remaining sin in his life he will never be a perfect example to his wife. He will fail—that much is certain. However, as Wayne Mack writes, 'Even in failure, the husband must be an example to his wife of how a believer should deal with sin.'[13] In other words, he will recognize his failings and he will confess those failings both to God and to his wife.

Men, how do you measure up to the biblical view of leadership? Young men, let me challenge you. If you are not prepared to try to be the sort of husband God wants you to be, don't enter into the sacred marriage bond and put some young lady through the misery of a bad marriage.

We have seen how wives are to submit to their husbands. We have seen how husbands are to exercise loving leadership over their wives. Let me ask you this: What is submission? Is it not a voluntary giving of yourself to someone else? And what does it mean to love? Does it not involve voluntarily giving yourself to someone else, as Christ gave himself for the church?[14]

That husbands are to be the leaders in the home is clear from Scripture. Leading involves making decisions, and sometimes those decisions will be unpopular. But no leader will ignore the suggestions or advice of the helper that God has given him. Therefore, no husband should ignore the advice of a godly wife. However, neither will he abdicate his responsibility to her. He is to be the leader of his family; he is accountable to God for the manner in which he leads, ensuring that he is not merely following his wife. What a challenge we face! Let's be honest: as husbands we are failing miserably. But, by God's grace and a determination to put God's Word into practice, we can at least begin to address the issue and cultivate the sort of loving leadership that God intends us to have in our homes.

I started this chapter with the heading 'Mission impossible!' Let me now close with that thought. Shortly after my wife Ela and I returned from our honeymoon, a friend of mine who is a pastor in Northern Ireland sent me an e-mail. In it he wrote, 'Marriage as God intended is not only difficult, it is impossible.' He was meaning that, although it is impossible to love our wives as Christ loved the church, yet by God's grace and in his strength that is exactly what we must strive for.

Husbands, are you ready for the impossible?

Study questions

FOR DISCUSSION

1. What does Ephesians 5:25 teach us about headship in the home?
2. Discuss Dr Jay Adams' term, 'loving leadership'.
3. Read Colossians 3:19.
   (a) What does this verse teach us about leadership in the home?
   (b) Husbands, make a list of at least five ways in which you can apply this principle.
4. Read Ephesians 5:28–33. In what practical ways can a husband love his wife as he loves his own body?
5. Try to summarize in one word what it means for a husband to love his wife as Christ loved the church.
6. Read 1 Peter 3:7. In what practical ways can a husband live in an 'understanding way' with his wife?

FOR PERSONAL REFLECTION

7. How do you measure up to the biblical view of leadership? Do you need to change? If so, are you prepared to change at least one area of your life today?

Notes

1 See **John Stott**, *The Message of Ephesians* (Leicester: IVP, 1979), p. 234.

2 **Palmer,** *The Family,* p. 31.

3 **Adams,** *Christian Living in the Home*, pp. 87–102.

4 Ibid. p. 25.

5 πικραίνεσθε from πικραίνω.

6 See **Rienecker,** *Linguistic Key to the Greek New Testament* (Grand Rapids: Zondervan, 1976), p. 582.

7 **Palmer,** p. 37.

8 **Calvin,** *Commentaries* (Ephesians) (Grand Rapids: Baker Book House, 1998), p. 322.

9 **Albert Barnes,** *Barnes on the New Testament*, vol. 57: *Ephesians–Colossians* (Blackie and Son, n. d.), p. 40.

10 **Mack,** *Strengthening Your Marriage*, p. 27.

11 κατὰ γνῶσιν 'Here it means greater Christian insight and tact, a conscious sensitivity to God's will' (**Rienecker,** *Linguistic Key to the New Testament* (Grand Rapids: Zondervan, 1976), p. 757).

12 **Dr James Dobson,** *What Wives wish their Husbands knew about Women* (Living Books, 1975), Chapter 7.

13 **Mack,** p. 29.

14 **Adams,** *Christian Living in the Home*, p. 235.

Responsibilities of children to parents

Children, obey your parents in the Lord, for this is right. Honor your father and mother (which is the first commandment with a promise), that it may be well with you, and that you may live long on the earth (Ephesians 6:1–3).

Honor your father and your mother, that your days may be prolonged in the land which the LORD your God gives you (Exodus 20:12).

A conflict of wills!

When he was a young boy Nastradini was very naughty. Whatever his father told him to do, Nastradini did the opposite. His father, unable to break this habit, was in the end compelled to employ some reverse psychology and say the opposite of what he wanted, so that Nastradini would then inadvertently do what his father did want.

One day, as the two were making their way home from the miller's, they had to cross a river. Even though there was a bridge, the donkey, which was laden with flour, did not want to cross over it. As Nastradini made towards the water's edge with the donkey, his father called out, 'Son, just one piece of advice: be sure to cross where the water is deep!'

Of course Nastradini did exactly what his father 'didn't want', and began to cross at a place where the water was shallow. Nevertheless, the flour sack on one side of the donkey began to touch the water. His father, seeing from the bridge what was happening and thinking that Nastradini would do the opposite of what he said, called out, 'Son, raise up the sack on your side and balance it with the other.'

Nastradini, realizing the seriousness of the situation, called back, 'Father, up to now I have always done the opposite of what you have told me. Now I'm going to do exactly as you say and see how it goes!' Having said this, Nastradini proceeded to raise higher the sack on his side of the donkey. This inevitably caused the donkey to overbalance and tumble with its load into the river.

Nastradini is not alone in finally discovering that parents actually know something after all. For many young people this realization comes at the end of a long period of insisting on doing things their own way despite the best advice of their parents. Of course, it doesn't have to be this way. Despite the contemporary culture of young people doing things their own way, it is possible for them to listen to their parents and to learn something from them.

In the next two chapters I want to address the issue of parent–child relationships. We will look at the specific responsibilities that children have towards their parents and those which parents have towards their children. I do not pretend to be an authority on these matters, therefore all I will simply try to do is open up to you the biblical principles involved in this relationship.

Little sinners

Jay Adams, in his book *Christian Living in the Home*, has written that good relationships between sinful children and sinful parents do not develop naturally.[1] They need to be worked at. Essentially this means that parents must give sufficient and quality time to their children.

The story is told of a very busy pastor who, while playing with his small son, received a phone call from one of his church members. Instantly he left his son and went to talk with the church member on the phone. After some time the pastor returned to find that his son, having been disappointed by the interruption, had gone on to do other things. This pastor learned the hard way that he needed to guard his time with his family. Following this incident he learned to respond to such phone calls firstly by ascertaining whether or not the matter was truly urgent, and then by telling the caller that he was with someone else and would return the call later. By taking this simple step his wife and children got the message that they were important to him. They felt loved and valued.

It has often been said, and I believe there to be no small amount of truth in it, that parents would have less need to lecture if they only took time to be with their children and to listen to them. However, a child should not be allowed to 'rule' the home through his or her demands for attention. It is common in our day for children constantly to demand more of their parents' attention, to the point where work or conversation between grown-ups is constantly interrupted and becomes almost impossible to sustain. Children know how to manipulate their parents and to get what they want. 'Crocodile tears' are a favourite weapon to ensure that they get their parents' full attention; disruptive behaviour is another. This is simply evidence of their fallen nature. It is therefore essential that children are taught from early on to have a proper respect for their parents. Dr James Dobson, a well-known child psychologist and professor of paediatrics at University of Southern California School of Medicine, puts it like this:

There is a critical period during the first four or five years of a child's life, when he can be taught proper attitudes. These early concepts become rather permanent. When the opportunity of those years is missed, however, the prime receptivity usually vanishes, never to return. If it is desirable that children be kind, appreciative, and pleasant, those qualities should be taught, not hoped for.[2]

I make no apology for asserting that children are sinners who instinctively desire to do wrong. They therefore need to be taught to know the difference between right and wrong, and, of course, to do that which is right. It may be difficult to believe or accept this truth, especially when you see the joy that a newly born child brings to the parents. It is a hard man indeed whose heart is not melted when for the first time he carefully takes that small, delicate bundle in his huge hands. How many doting fathers have looked at that small face for the first time and whispered affectionately, 'My little angel!' What father do you know who has picked up his child for the first time and welcomed it into this world with the words, 'My little sinner'?

And yet, that's exactly what that wonderful, precious gift from God is: a little sinner. David says in Psalm 51:5, 'Behold, I was brought forth in iniquity, and in sin my mother conceived me.' This psalm is, of course, David's recognition of his own inherent sinfulness from the perspective of parenthood (following his adultery with Bathsheba). Nevertheless, it is a clear statement that every one of us has entered this world with a corrupt nature—and that includes that little bundle of joy held on a parent's lap. As Matthew Henry puts it, 'We have from our birth the snares of sin in our bodies, the seeds of sin in our souls, and the stain of sin upon both. This is what we call original sin …'[3] When we recognize this fundamental fact, we will have no problem accepting that the best way to address that sin, and the best way to raise our children, is by the application of biblical principles.

In this chapter we will look at two things the Bible has to say to children and teenagers. The first is found in Exodus 20:12, the fifth commandment, where we read, 'Honor your father and your mother, that your days may be prolonged in the land which the LORD your God gives you.' The first command given to children, therefore, is that they should honour their parents. The second command flows from the first and it is found in Ephesians 6:1 and Colossians 3:20. It is 'Children, obey your parents …'

So closely related are honour and obedience that in Ephesians 6 Paul qualifies his command 'to obey' by quoting from the fifth commandment. However, for the sake of clarity we will look at the two separately.

Honour

Firstly, then, children are to honour their parents. The Hebrew word translated 'honour' in Exodus 20:12 is *kabad*.[4] It has the root meaning of 'to be heavy'. In the bad sense it can mean 'to be a burden', 'insensible' or 'stupid'. But in the good sense the word means 'to be numerous', 'wealthy' or 'honourable'.[5]

Sometimes when we refer to people who have a lot of influence, we say that they 'carry a lot of weight', meaning quite simply that they are influential. For example, a consultant surgeon is a doctor who is at the top of his or her profession and who therefore has a lot of influence—his or her word 'carries a lot of weight'. Now imagine that you or a member of your family is ill and you go to the hospital for examination. If the consultant surgeon says you need an operation to save your life, do you think for a moment that you will argue with the surgeon and say, 'I don't need an operation, don't be silly'? Of course not! In fact, one of the first things that you will ask the doctor is, 'When can I have the operation?' The point I am making is that you do not naturally question the surgeon's advice; instead, because of the surgeon's years of experience, you accept his or her word. It 'carries weight' and is to be respected or honoured. In the same way, children are to honour their parents. Because parents have had years of experience that children have not yet had, their advice 'carries weight', and should be respected or honoured.

Let's look at this from another angle. What do you think of when I mention the word 'curse'? To help you answer that question, look at Exodus 21:17: 'He who curses his father or his mother shall surely be put to death' (see also Leviticus 20:9). What do you think it means for a son to 'curse' his father or mother? The *Oxford English Dictionary* defines 'curse' as (a) 'A solemn utterance intended to invoke a supernatural power to inflict destruction or punishment on a person or thing' or (b) 'A violent exclamation of anger'. Now that's fairly strong language. To curse someone according to this definition involves the use of strong language and unpleasant desires. But what does the Hebrew word teach us?

The actual Hebrew word used is *qalal*[6] and it means 'to be light' or 'to cause something to be light', 'slight', 'trifling' or 'insignificant'. In other words, simply to treat your parents in a 'light' or 'trifling' manner, or to treat what they say as insignificant and simply do your own thing with no thought for them, is, according to the Hebrew word *qalal*, 'to curse' your parents.

Admittedly the verb for 'curse' used in Exodus 21:17 is in the Hebrew Piel form. Simply stated, this indicates that the writer has in mind intense and intentional disregard for one's parents. The context of the passage makes it clear that cursing parents was on a par with hitting or striking them—both being punishable by death. I must also hasten to add that the form of the verb used here is the participle, which expresses continuous mistreatment of parents. In Leviticus 20:9 the same word, used in the same context, is in the imperfect form, also expressing a continued action. In other words, not every child who was disobedient to his or her parents was put to death. If that were the case it is likely that no children would have survived childhood, and the Jewish nation would have ceased to exist. Rather, the verb speaks of continuous, habitual mistreatment of parents that brought dishonour upon them.[7]

Everyone, adults as well as children, can and does make mistakes. We all sin in our treatment of others. But if we see our wrong and confess our sin then, thankfully, there is forgiveness with God. The same was undoubtedly true of children in Old Testament times and if, for example, an offending son admitted his sin, forgiveness was freely available. Nevertheless, it is very clear that God treated simple indifference towards parents as a very serious offence indeed. Therefore he says, 'Do not "make light" of your parents.' Rather, treat them as people who carry a lot of weight; treat them with respect, honour them. To honour your parents is to adhere to, agree to or abide by what is right, or to agree to the standard of conduct that they decide is appropriate for their home.

In God's eyes, dishonouring parents, even by simply dismissing what they say or treating what they say lightly, is considered to be committing sin as serious as idolatry and other terrible sins (see Leviticus 20).

Obey

Secondly, children are to 'obey' their parents. In Ephesians 6:1 we find that Paul uses the word *hupakouo*.[8] This word is also in the imperative form; it is an order. Paul is not suggesting that it might be a good idea for children to obey their parents. He is not simply implying that if you obey your parents it will avoid a lot of unnecessary arguments in the home. Paul is not reasoning with children here.

So much of secular psychology would have us believe that children should not be forced to do anything they do not want to do. Parents are told to treat their children as adults and, when the children misbehave, to simply sit down and talk 'man to man' with them, rather than punish them. We are told that a parent must never demand or force a child to conform to any rules. Now at this point it is necessary to bring some balance to the issue at hand and to be careful not to overstate the case. While there is a divine imperative to obedience, in practical terms a parent must not allow that to become a licence for authoritarianism. We will consider this further in the next chapter. Nevertheless, God does command children to honour their parents.

Such obedience is not an optional extra. We cannot choose to obey only when we want to. God's Word makes it clear. Children, obey your parents! When children or teenagers disobey their parents, they are in fact also disobeying God.

It is also worth noting that, in contrast to common ideas about the child–parent relationship, the onus is placed upon children to obey. It is not only parents but also children who are given a responsibility. Now let me challenge any young person who may be reading this book: What will you do with that responsibility, and how will you act upon it? Will you prove yourself faithful in the small things with which God entrusts you, or will you be like the servant with one talent (Matthew 25:14–30)?

How? And why?

For the remainder of this chapter I want to address two questions. The first is: How?—in what manner are children to obey? The second is: Why are children to obey their parents?

For the first question we can learn a very simple lesson from the Greek word used. We have already seen that the verb is in the imperative—that it is a command. But the verb is also in the present tense. This indicates that obedience is something to be done now, in the present. It was not only for a time in the past, nor is it something to think about for the future. Paul commands children to be obedient *now*. Furthermore, the verb is made up from two Greek words: *hupo*, meaning 'under', and *akouo*, meaning 'to hear' or 'to listen'. It therefore has the very basic idea of 'listening to' or 'paying attention to' someone.

Sadly, in our day there are many young people who turn their backs on their parents or interrupt them when they are still talking to them. Young people, when your parents are talking to you, listen to them; pay attention to them. If you want to reply to something that they are saying, be patient. Wait until they have finished talking and then, in a manner that will not dishonour them nor 'make light' of what they are saying, share your thoughts and concerns with them.

At this point I want to draw your attention back to the word 'honour'. To 'honour' someone or something has the idea of 'holding fast' to what is right or to a particular standard of conduct. Young people, you may not like some of the rules that your parents have in the home. You may not like having to be in by 8.30 or 9 pm, but while you are still living under your parents' roof you should 'hold firmly' to the standard of conduct that they desire in the home.

To the best of your ability you should try to keep their rules.

And older (or should I say, more mature) people: Do you realize that as long as your parents are still alive, you are still to honour them? Of course, as we saw in Chapter 2, when a man leaves his father and mother and cleaves to a wife, the parents' authority does not extend to the new family unit. Nevertheless, you should still honour and respect your parents in every way you can. For example, when you return to your parents' home, even for a short visit, you should honour them by accepting the standard of conduct that they set in their home.

There are limitations, of course. In Ephesians 6:1–4 we read these two commands: 'Children, obey your parents in the Lord', and 'Fathers … bring them [your children] up in the discipline and instruction of the Lord'. As B. M. Palmer puts it, 'If the children must "obey in the Lord", the parent must command in the Lord…', and, 'If the child must obey as "well pleasing to the Lord", the parent is equally to please the Lord in his rule.'[9]

'Well,' you might say, 'that's fine if both parents and children are Christians and the Word of God is the guide for both. But what should a Christian child do if the parents are not Christians?' The answer is very simple: you should still obey your parents 'in all things', as Paul exhorts in Colossians 3:20. The only exceptions are if your parents tell you to do something that God has told you not to do, or if they tell you not to do something that God has commanded you to do. Apart from this, children should obey their parents in all things.

Now let's attempt to answer a child's favourite question: 'Why?' Why should children obey their parents? I will give you four answers to that question; there may well be many more.

Firstly, children should obey their parents simply because it is right. How many times have you heard a child ask its dad, 'Why?' And occasionally a very patient dad will take time to explain the reason for a particular event or course of action. Immediately the dad has finished his explanation, the child simply asks again, 'But why, Daddy?' And so the 'conversation' continues to the point where the father, having been asked 'why?' for the hundredth time, simply says, 'Because that's the way it is!' The implication is that it is simply the right thing to do.

Look again at Ephesians 6:1. Paul says, 'Children, obey your parents in the Lord, *for this is right*' (emphasis mine). Paul doesn't offer any other reasons here. He does not apply the psychology of the world and go to great lengths to explain the command of obedience. He simply says, 'This is right!'

Secondly, obedience to parents brings pleasure, and exhibits wisdom on the part of the child or young person. Proverbs 10:1 says, 'A wise son makes a father glad, but a foolish son is a grief to his mother.' It is a wise son who listens to his father's advice or pays attention to his father. Such obedience is naturally pleasing to a parent. Obedience also brings pleasure to God. Do you remember how Jesus fulfilled 'all righteousness' when he was baptized by John the Baptist in the river Jordan, and how immediately the heavens were opened and God said, 'This is My beloved Son, in whom I am well-pleased' (Matthew 3:15–17)? Jesus' obedience pleased God, and your obedience pleases God! In Colossians 3:20 Paul writes, 'Children, be obedient to your parents in all things, *for this is well-pleasing to the Lord*' (emphasis mine).

Thirdly, Christ exemplifies obedience to parents. In Luke 2:51 we read, 'And He went down with them, and came to Nazareth; and he continued in subjection to them; and His mother treasured all these things in her heart.' This passage tells us how Jesus was subject to his human father and mother. He obeyed his parents. John Angell James puts it like this: 'That wonderful person, God manifest in the flesh, was subject, we have reason to believe, to his parents, till at the age of thirty he entered his public ministry.'[10]

Young person, are you a follower of Christ? Are you prepared to follow his example of obedience to parents?

Finally, obedience to parents brings blessing. The prophet Jeremiah wrote these words:

Then Jeremiah said to the house of the Rechabites, 'Thus says the LORD of hosts, the God of Israel, "Because you have obeyed the command of Jonadab your father, kept all his commands, and done according to all that he commanded you; therefore thus says the LORD of hosts, the God of Israel, 'Jonadab the son of Rechab shall not lack a man to stand before [or serve] Me always'"' (Jeremiah 35:18–19).

This passage refers to an extraordinary instance of obedience that had continued in one family over a period of 300 years. The Rechabites had been forbidden by their father to drink wine, and they obeyed him. For their obedience, God praised them.[11] This is in keeping with the fifth commandment, which Paul calls the first commandment with a promise (Ephesians 6:2–3). There are other instances in the Scriptures that could be quoted on this point,[12] but it is enough to repeat that obedience to parents brings blessing to both parents and child.

Young people, are you prepared to be a barrier to that blessing? Or are you going to reach out for that blessing in joyful obedience to your parents? Don't be like Nastradini, of whom we read at the beginning of this chapter. Don't leave your obedience until it's too late. Don't make light of your parents; rather treat them as those whose word carries weight. Honour God and your parents by your willing obedience now.

Study questions

FOR DISCUSSION

1. Upon what biblical basis can we assert that rebelliousness, even in small children, is the result of sin?
2. Discuss this statement: 'It has often been said that parents would have less need to lecture if they only took time to be with their children and listen to them.'
3. Why is it so important to teach proper attitudes and manners to children under four years of age?
4. In what practical ways can children (even grown-up children) honour their parents?
5. Read Ephesians 6:1–4.
   (a) What light does this passage shed on how children are to obey their parents?
   (b) Discuss practical ways in which a child should obey his or her parents.
6. Read Ephesians 6:1–4, Colossians 3:20 and Proverbs 10:1. According to these passages, why should children obey their parents?

FOR PERSONAL REFLECTION

7. How much do you love and respect your parents? In what practical ways

Chapter 8

can you show your respect for your parents?

Notes

1 **Adams,** *Christian Living in the Home*, p. 104.

2 **Dr James Dobson,** *Dare to Discipline* (Tyndale House Publishers, 1970), p. 20.

3 **Matthew Henry,** *Commentary on the Whole Bible*, vol. 3 (Macdonald Publishing Company, n. d.), p. 431.

4 כָּבֵד or כָּבַד (kabad or kabed), with the basic meaning to be heavy, or burdensome.

5 See *Strong's Exhaustive Concordance* (Grand Rapids: Baker Book House, 1989), p. 490, which is linked to *Gesenius' Hebrew-Chaldee Lexicon to the Old Testament* (Grand Rapids: Baker Book House, 1979) (Strong's Number 3513), p.381.

6 קלל See **William L. Holladay** (ed.), *A Concise Hebrew and Aramaic Lexicon of the Old Testament* (Grand Rapids: Eerdmans, 1988), p. 318.

7 See **Keil and Delitzsch,** *Commentary on the Old Testament* (Grand Rapids: Eerdmans, 1991), vol. 1, p. 133.

8 ὑπακούετε. This verb is in the imperative present active 2nd person plural.

9 **Palmer,** *The Family*, p. 112.

10 **James,** *A Help to Domestic Happiness*, p. 200.

11 See further **Thomas Watson,** *The Ten Commandments* (Edinburgh: Banner of Truth, 1990), p. 130.

12 See Proverbs 4:1ff for the blessings upon the child, and Proverbs 23:15, 24–25 for the blessings upon the parent.

Responsibilities of parents to children

And, fathers, do not provoke your children to anger; but bring them up in the discipline and instruction of the Lord (Ephesians 6:4).

Fathers, do not exasperate your children, that they may not lose heart (Colossians 3:21).

Before operation, carefully read the instructions

I'm sure that on occasions you have received a beautifully wrapped gift. Knowing that it was a particularly special gift, you would have begun carefully to remove the wrapping and open the box. Before you could remove the gift itself, you might have found a small piece of paper with instructions on how to care for your new product.

A typical example of this is when you buy a new washing machine. You are told to read the instructions carefully before using the machine. There is packaging in all the most awkward places, not to mention screws or bolts to be removed before use, and you follow the instructions because you know that improper use can result in the machine being broken.

Psalm 127:3–5 says, 'Behold, children are a gift of the Lord; the fruit of the womb is a reward. Like arrows in the hand of a warrior, so are the children of one's youth. How blessed is the man whose quiver is full of them …' The meaning of this passage is self-evident: children are a gift from God; indeed, it would almost intimate that the more, the merrier. Contrary to common thinking that children are little accidents of nature, the Word of God makes it clear that they are his special gift to parents. John Calvin put it like this: 'The meaning then is, that children are not the fruit of chance, but that God, as it seems good to him, distributes to every man his share of them.'[1]

Perhaps a word of clarification is necessary at this point. Some couples, despite having a great desire to have children, remain childless. It is with great sensitivity and pastoral concern that I mention this; I do not want in any way to add to their sense of disappointment. Indeed, at the time of writing this very section my wife and I were experiencing just such disappointment. Children are indeed a blessing from the Lord, as indicated above, but if we are to believe that, we must likewise believe the Word of God when it teaches us that barrenness is also from the Lord. In 1 Samuel 1:4–5 we read, 'And when the day came that Elkanah sacrificed, he would give portions to Peninnah his wife and to all her sons and her daughters; but to Hannah he would give a double portion, for he loved Hannah, but the LORD had closed her womb.'

In most situations the Lord blesses couples with children, but in some instances God sovereignly chooses not to. In the passage quoted from 1 Samuel it is the Lord who has closed Hannah's womb and withheld children from her. This has nothing to do with Hannah's suitability or unsuitability as a parent (later the Lord opens her womb and blesses her with a child), nor is she being punished by God for some unmentioned sin. Indeed, we see later in the same passage that Hannah was a God-fearing woman. Couples who are trying to have children must never be led to think that they are being punished or that they are somehow not suitable for parenthood just because God has (at least for the time being) decided to withhold that special privilege from them. As the apostle Paul learned the secret of contentment, so childless couples can learn the secret of contentment through Christ, who gives strength sufficient to all our needs (Philippians 4:11–13). To say this is in no way to detract from the very real sense of disappointment, but simply to suggest that in trusting God we must learn to trust him in all things, even when life hurts.[2]

Children, then, are a gift and a blessing from the Lord, but without undermining this wonderful biblical truth I have to say that, on occasions, parents may be caused to wonder what the blessing is. How many mothers have been driven to the point of despair by hyperactive children racing around the room and demanding attention by getting up to all sorts of mischief? How many mums and dads, who, after a hard day's work just want to relax and listen to some music, or enjoy that well-earned cup of tea, instead find themselves having to jump out of the armchair repeatedly to take their child away from potential danger? When moments like these are multiplied, even the most caring parent must occasionally wonder where the blessing is. Nevertheless, children are a heritage from the Lord. They are a gift, a wonderful and precious gift; and like most precious gifts they do not come without instructions on how to care for them. But how many young couples embark upon parenthood without 'reading the instructions'? Before they know it, the 'machine' (the parent-child relationship) is damaged due to misuse.

In this chapter, I want to consider some of the biblical dos and don'ts of parenthood. I want to look at the instructions that God has left with parents to enable them to care for the gift he has given them. There are many passages in Scripture that refer to this subject, but I think it is fair to say that God, in his wisdom, has captured the essence of all the other passages in just one verse, Ephesians 6:4, where we read, 'Fathers, do not provoke your children to anger; but bring them up in the discipline and instruction of the Lord.'

Here the apostle Paul makes it very clear that parents are to bring up their children. It is not something to be left to other authorities, as we shall see below. Parental instruction is here set out in both negative and positive forms. Negatively, Paul says, '*Don't* provoke your children.' Positively, he says, '*Do* train them, and *do* instruct them.' Let's look at Paul's positive instructions first of all, which are twofold: discipline and instruction.

Forms of discipline

Although Paul uses two different words here—*paideia* (discipline) and *nouthesia* (instruction)—these words are not mutually exclusive. To some extent they overlap in their meaning, in that they both have the idea of educating, training or disciplining a child.[3] Yet each word highlights a different emphasis in what it means to educate, train or discipline.

PUNISHMENT AS A FORM OF DISCIPLINE

The Greek word *paideia*,[4] for example, refers in a general sense to the whole training and education of children.[5] It includes the idea of caring for a child's physical needs (feeding and clothing them, etc.), as well as of simply teaching them the difference between right and wrong. However, the word *paideia* also includes the idea of reproving and punishing. Fritz Rienecker, in his analysis of this word, says that '[it] indicates the discipline used to correct transgressions of the laws and ordinances of the Christian household.'[6]

There are those who suggest that children under three years of age do not fully understand the idea of right and wrong; that they see themselves as the centre of the universe and therefore behave as if their own immediate needs are more important than anything else. This sort of selfish behaviour is said to be normal in the under-three.

In response to this I want to mention a few things: firstly, it is absolutely true that a child below the age of three cannot be expected to know faultlessly the difference between right and wrong. My mother used to say, and rightly so, that 'you cannot put an old head on young shoulders'. A small child cannot be expected to understand concepts that even some adults still do not understand. Secondly, it is true that selfish behaviour is absolutely normal in small children. Such behaviour is the normal outward expression of a small heart and mind that are affected by sin. However, because it is normal, it does not mean that it is acceptable. Even in the toddler years (indeed, especially in the toddler years) it is the parent's duty to begin the long and difficult process of teaching a child the difference between right and wrong. It has often been said, 'Give me a boy to the age of seven and I will give you the man.' The idea is that children are more impressionable and receptive to instruction in their earliest years and therefore it is then that is the best time to instil in them Christian morals and virtues. Sometimes, as we shall see a little later in the study, this will involve nothing more than a gentle reminder of the difference between right and wrong, but other times it will involve the use of the 'encourager' or 'rod'.

Few parenting issues inflame the emotions as much as the issue of spanking children. Parents are strongly divided on the issue. There are those who believe that spanking is an important means of discipline, while others argue against it on the grounds that spanking, or corporal punishment in general, simply teaches children to be aggressive and may cause psychological harm. There is no definite scientific evidence either way, and certainly no evidence from either side of the argument that is not strongly biased.

What we as Christians need to remember is that we are looking for God's prescription for a healthy family, so let's see what his Word says. There are many passages, especially in Proverbs, to which we might turn for teaching on this theme. I have selected just a few to make the point.

- 'He who spares his rod hates his son, but he who loves him disciplines him diligently' (Proverbs 13:24).
- 'Stern discipline is for him who forsakes the way; he who hates reproof will die. Sheol and Abaddon lie open before the Lord, how much more the hearts of men!' (Proverbs 15:10–11).
- 'Do not hold back discipline from the child, although you beat him with the rod, he will not die' (Proverbs 23:13).

At this point it is necessary for me to explain what is meant by 'the rod' in the passages quoted above. Some object that, because this is mentioned in the wisdom literature of the Bible, the term 'rod' is not to be understood literally but in a figurative sense. Some theologians suggest that such teachings on the use of the rod in Proverbs should be simply culturally defined: that they applied to a culture where society had no social workers, probation officers or organized police force to maintain the law. In that culture, they suggest, these proverbs reflected the cultural idea of parental authority, and the necessary measures for parents to maintain discipline. It is my belief that to reason in this way is very dangerous indeed in the society in which we live today. In no small measure it clearly suggests an abdication of parental responsibility to the local authorities. It seems to me to suggest that the correct discipline and training of a child in our modern society lies not in the hands of the parents, but in the hands of the schools, social services and, where the circumstances are sufficiently severe, the local police force and judicial system. This is indeed far removed from the biblical standard that asserts that the primary training of a child is the responsibility of that child's parents.

It therefore seems to me that 'the rod' can legitimately be translated into our modern culture as the parent's open hand applied to the child's bottom or to the back of the child's hand. I am not advocating the use of a literal rod; nevertheless the punishment must be real, and the offender ought to feel the sting of it, the sting of pain for wrong behaviour. On the other hand, the punishment should not be excessive so as to actually injure the child.

Allow me to quickly qualify what I have just said in case any are tempted to think that I am endorsing an unqualified level of discipline:

CHILD ABUSE IS TO BE ABHORRED AND REJECTED
In days when there seems to be increasing cruelty to children, I want to make it absolutely clear that I do not endorse, in any way, any form of cruelty, neglect or mistreatment of children.

Children are a blessing from the Lord and as such ought to be treasured, respected and nurtured with all the love and compassion any parent can muster.

To talk of disciplining a child with an appropriate measure of discipline—which includes the possible need for some form of corporal punishment such as spanking—is very different from a wilful or even careless abuse of such discipline. *Physical abuse of children at the hands of grown-ups is radically different from biblical discipline, and is to be abhorred, rejected and, if possible, eradicated from society.*

Even Christian parents, who are seeking to apply biblical discipline to their children, must be very careful not to enter the arena of abuse. They ought never to discipline unnecessarily, too frequently or too severely. They must never allow the legitimate use of biblical discipline to become an excuse for unnecessary punishment or simply a means of venting their own anger or frustration. The Bible clearly teaches that part of the fruit of the Spirit (Galatians 5) is self-control, and this applies as much in the whole realm of disciplining children as in any other area of the Christian life. Mistreatment of children is one of the great evils of today's world, and God has set himself against those who do evil (see Psalm 34:15–16 and Peter's use of this psalm in 1 Peter 3:10–12). Nevertheless, it is clear from Scripture that in the course of training their children, parents may have to use corporal punishment, perhaps in the form of spanking the child's bottom.

CHILDREN MUST BE ALLOWED TO EXPLORE THEIR FIVE SENSES
Having worked with children of all ages and in different contexts, one thing

I have learned is that children all differ from one another in many ways. For many children, discipline will involve nothing more than a stern look, even sometimes merely a disappointed look, from a person they respect. In the family context it is my sincere belief that many spankings may actually be avoided if parents can only learn to recognize their children's genuine tendency to explore their five senses and the environment in which they live, which often leads to small accidents with mum's most precious ornaments. One of the first things that parents need to learn to discern in their toddler is the vital distinction between a child's real fears and concerns, curiosity and even a natural proneness to small accidents, and the outright rebellion of which every toddler is capable.

So, what do the three passages quoted above teach us about the use of a rod (as defined above) in discipline? We can see that they teach us that it is a legitimate form of discipline, but in addition they teach us at least three other basic truths.

Firstly, they teach us that a proper use of the rod is actually an expression of love. For the modern mindset that may seem to be a contradiction, but nevertheless that is what God's Word says. 'He who spares his rod hates his son.'

Secondly, we see that a proper use of the rod may actually help in delivering your child from hell and destruction (Proverbs 15:10–11).

Thirdly, we learn that proper use of the rod will not kill the child nor in any way injure him or her.

We saw in a previous chapter how it is the husband's responsibility to lead the home. I have to say that I have been in homes where it was not the husband who led the family, nor was it the wife: they were ruled by the five-, six- or ten-year-old child. I have seen mums and dads sit down after a hard day's work to watch a television programme, and their small child kick and scream until they changed to the cartoon channel. I have seen parents all dressed up to go out for the evening together, with the babysitter ready to look after the children, and their child kick and scream until the parents decide to stay at home. Fathers, you are the head of your household; you are the king in your castle, so to speak. Don't allow a five-year-old 'Absalom' to snap the sceptre from your hand or to bring you grief and despair.[7] Rather, as Proverbs 29:17 tells us, 'Correct your son, and he will give you comfort.'

At this point, some parents may react by thinking, 'Surely putting the child to bed without supper may be just as effective as the rod.' Well, I have two things to say in response to that. Firstly, parents are duty-bound to meet the practical needs of their children, and that includes providing food when they are hungry. Secondly, this method is not sanctioned in Scripture. In fact, it is not that far removed (in principle) from what David did to Absalom. We read in 2 Samuel 13 how Absalom murdered his brother Amnon for dishonouring their sister Tamar. Then we are told that Absalom fled (v. 34) from David, knowing that the penalty for murder was death. Now, David made no attempt to 'discipline' Absalom in the correct manner. He allowed Absalom to 'stay in his room' (in the sense that he stayed with his grandfather for three years, v. 37). Eventually David's heart softened towards Absalom, who was then allowed to return to the royal household. And how did Absalom repay David's leniency? We read that he conspired to snatch the kingdom from David, and their relationship was even worse than before.

Death, of course, is a rather unusual and extreme form of discipline. I hasten to mention that, although death was warranted in ancient Israel for children who cursed or dishonoured their parents, there is no record of it actually being applied in the Old Testament. Perhaps the reason for that was in no small part due to exhortations and teachings such as that found in Proverbs 19:18, where we read, 'Discipline your son while there is hope, and do not desire his death.' Proper corrective discipline was actually designed to prevent the ultimate penalty of death, and it would appear that in ancient Israel it proved quite effective. 'Correct your son'—discipline your son—'and he will give you comfort' (Proverbs 29:17); whereas 'a child who gets his own way brings shame to his mother' (Proverbs 29:15).

Parents, the rod, correctly applied and never to be abused, is a legitimate and divinely approved method of disciplining your child. However, the rod is not the only method, nor indeed the *primary* method, for disciplining a child.

ENCOURAGEMENT AS A FORM OF DISCIPLINE

Discipline ought to be employed in proportion to the severity of the misdemeanour committed. What every parent needs to bear in mind is that discipline, especially of younger children, is actually made easier by the child's dependence upon Mum and Dad, and that dependence extends to the child's need to know when a father or mother is pleased with him or her. Therefore, discipline can take the form of encouragement. Children of all ages love to be told they have done well. Small children love to be cuddled and praised by their parents. Parents ought, therefore, to cuddle their children regularly as an outward expression of their love for them. This will go a long way to making discipline much easier, and less frequently needed.

Simply encouraging children when they do well can be a very effective tool in the hands of parents. This comes out in the second word that Paul uses in Ephesians 6:4, *nouthesia*.[8] Rienecker says that this word refers to training by word, and, when it is sufficient, a word of encouragement. It ought to be recognized that gentle pressure or persuasion over a period of time can steer a child's will better than the 'sledgehammer' approach. B. M. Palmer puts it beautifully when he says, 'The idea is not to break that will, but to educate it, not to bind its freedom by external force, but to teach it to control itself.'[9]

Parents have an average of eighteen years to discipline or educate their children, and it is a wise parent indeed who uses this time to advantage. Ancient history tells us of army commanders who, recognizing that some ancient strongholds or cities could never be taken by a full-frontal attack, with patience and time brought those same cities or strongholds to capitulate or willingly submit after a long siege. In the same way, they are wise parents who choose their battles and recognize that some battles will never be won by a full-frontal attack; who, over a period of time, steer their children by gentle persuasion and by appealing to their ever-increasing understanding. Use the tool of encouragement to its utmost in gently persuading your child of the benefits of doing the right thing.

Discipline, then, can take the form of punishment, encouragement or gentle persuasion. But perhaps one of the most neglected methods of disciplining a child is that of setting a godly example.

SETTING A GODLY EXAMPLE AS A MEANS OF DISCIPLINE

It is interesting that Christ did not simply say, 'Do as I say' or 'Do as I tell you'; rather, he said 'Follow me!' More specifically, in John 13:15 we read these words: 'For I gave you an example that you also should do as I have done for you.'

In this incident taken from the 'Upper Room discourse' we find that Jesus did not order one of the disciples to wash the feet of the others. Rather, he showed by example how we ought to serve one another and how we can best help one another.

In the same way, it is not enough for Dad to bark orders at the children to help their mother around the home. He should show by his example how the children can help their mum. It is not enough for Dad to rebuke a child for talking in an unkind way to Mum (or someone else, for that matter) if the children constantly hear Mum and Dad arguing. It is not enough to encourage a child to go to church meetings and to live in the fear of God if the parents are not seen to be walking in the fear of God.

A parent's relationship with God should not simply be sincere, it should also be visible! It ought to be seen by the children so that they can follow the example. Children always have their eyes upon their parents and they are quick to see inconsistency. John Angell James puts it like this: 'The first book [children] read … that which they continue to read, and by far the most influential, is that of their parents' example.'[10]

Instruction of the Lord

The apostle Paul takes this idea of personal religion a step further when he says that children are to be brought up in the 'instruction of the Lord' (Ephesians 6:4). It is good for parents to teach children to be well mannered, it is good to teach them social skills that will help them do well in life, but children are to receive the 'instruction of the Lord' so that they are prepared not only for this life, but also for the life to come.

Parents, ask yourself this serious and fundamental question: What will it benefit your children if they gain all the benefits that this world has to offer but lose their own souls (Matthew 16:26)? Make it your primary task as parents to instruct your children in the Word of God and to show them clearly the way of salvation to be found there.

If discipline in the sense of instruction or admonition is to be used, it necessarily involves training a child by means of rules and regulations. In 2

Timothy 3:16, the same word, *paideia*, is used in exactly this sense. There it refers to the Word of God as being profitable for teaching, reproof, correction and training in righteousness. It is the parents' responsibility to instruct their children in the Word of God. It is not something to be ignored or simply left to others. I will take up this subject again in Chapter 11.

The dos of parenthood are: train or discipline your children, and instruct them in the things of God. Now let's look at the don'ts of parenthood.

Faults to avoid

In Ephesians 6:4 Paul says, 'Do not provoke your children to anger.'

The language here is plain and simple, and it indicates that, on occasions, a child's rebelliousness or sense of hopelessness can actually be provoked or caused by the parents. Children are duty-bound to obey their parents, but, Calvin writes, 'parents, on the other hand, are exhorted not to irritate their children by unreasonable severity.'[11] Calvin goes on to assert that 'This would excite hatred, and would lead them to throw off the yoke altogether. Accordingly, in writing to the Colossians, he adds, "lest they be discouraged" (Colossians 3: 21.).'[12]

AVOID UNNECESSARY AND CONSTANT CRITICISM

I am aware of situations in Christian homes where parents have been so keen to maintain discipline and order in the home that they have overlooked this basic principle of not provoking their children to anger. One home had a rule that said that the teenage son had to be home by 10 pm; for teenagers that is a very reasonable request. However, if the son arrived home at 10.05 pm, he found the door bolted from the inside, which meant that he had to disturb the parents to open the door and let him in. This generally led to an immediate confrontation and argument. Obviously the parents felt justified in this action. After all, the son had broken a house rule. The son, on the other hand, felt that he was being punished unnecessarily. After all, he reasoned, he had walked home as quickly as possible, and had only missed the appointed time by five minutes. The parents would then reply that he should have left his friends five minutes earlier. The arguments and frustrations continued over the years, to the point where the parent–son relationship was severely damaged and the son became increasingly rebellious. This is a clear example of a son who 'lost heart' trying to please his parents, because, as he saw it, no matter what he did, it was not enough. 'Do not exasperate your children, that they may not lose heart' (Colossians 3:21).

There is nothing more disheartening for a child than to try to please his or her parents, only to discover that the parents focus upon his or her faults. Parents, without opening the floodgates for cleverly orchestrated rebellion subtly applied by an astute teenager, do make some allowance for the inconsistencies of youth.[13] Learn to distinguish between a child's natural capacity to fail, and open defiance: there is a big difference between the two. This will enable you to avoid unnecessary and constant criticism. If your teenager arrives home five minutes late, and you detect that it was a genuine mistake, commend him or her for not being ten minutes late. Constant criticism and unnecessary strictness is a sure recipe for the exasperation of children.

Aim also for consistency in your application of discipline. In other words, do not simply apply discipline according to your own mood at the time. That will inevitably lead to discipline being administered when it is perhaps not necessary, and not administered when it ought to be. It is up to you as a parent to set the ground rules, and to apply them consistently. Inconsistency in this area is another sure recipe for the exasperation of your child.

AVOID UNNECESSARY AND DISPARAGING COMPARISONS

Belittling comparisons can cause a child to lose heart. Constantly comparing your children's achievements, for example, with those of their friends or neighbours who are perhaps higher achievers, is a means of discouraging your child. Perhaps this is most clearly seen in how well a child is doing at school. Of course it is important to encourage children to do their best at school, but be careful not to cause a child to lose heart by constantly reminding him or her that the exam results are not as good as those of Johnny next door. This also applies within your family; for example, comparing one son's ability or behaviour with another son's ability or behaviour, or showing favouritism to one child, which causes another child to lose heart. How many parents make this mistake!

Excessive love and attention is poured out upon one child to the point where jealousy and resentment builds up in the hearts of the others.[14] Parents should avoid expressions of favouritism and comparisons that belittle within the family.

AVOID UNNECESSARY AND EXCESSIVE DISCIPLINE

Unnecessary or excessive discipline can exasperate a child or cause him or her to lose heart. I know a family situation where I believe this to be happening. When a boy does wrong, the father actually sends him to fetch the belt with which he is going to punish him, and if the boy does not go immediately for the belt, the punishment is increased. Even when the boy apologizes for the wrong done and pleads for mercy, the punishment is still carried out. Where would we be if God treated us like that? Not one of us would escape the fires of hell. Of course parents need to be careful that they are not manipulated by the child; nevertheless, where there is clear evidence of sorrow for wrongdoing, forgiveness should be extended to the child, not punishment.

AVOID PSYCHOLOGICAL TERROR AS A FORM OF DISCIPLINE

At this point I must denounce one further form of punishment or control that is sometimes used by parents: leaving the 'rod' or belt in a prominent place in the home as a reminder to the child to behave. In my opinion, that is nothing short of terrorism in the home. God does not command parents to terrorize their children, rather to 'bring them up in the discipline and instruction of the Lord'. There will not be a healthy atmosphere if children are living in constant fear of their next mistake. It will not be an atmosphere where they will develop as God intended. As B. M. Palmer puts it, 'It is doubtful if obedience ought ever to be enforced under a menace.'[15]

AVOID DISCIPLINING IN ANGER

Parents should avoid disciplining a child in anger. Often, discipline is executed for all the wrong reasons. A mother has reached the 'end of her tether', or a father is just too busy with that all-important piece of work that needs to be submitted to the boss by Friday. In each case tempers are easily frayed, and the breaking point comes when their child oversteps the mark yet again. Parents ought to avoid disciplining their child when they are angry because discipline under such circumstances is often stronger than it needs to be. Therefore it is better for parents to wait until they are calm before administering discipline.

AVOID 'DIVISION IN THE RANKS'
Parents should also avoid 'division in the ranks': Mum and Dad must be seen by children to be united on the issue of discipline. If parents are not united on this issue, they should discuss it privately and not in the hearing of the children. Do not give your children an opening to drive a wedge between you. Children are astute and can very quickly run to one parent for protection when they know they have done wrong and are expecting to be punished. They can very often play one parent off against the other. If parents are not united in the cause and method of rearing their children in an atmosphere of loving, corrective discipline, very quickly proper discipline in the home will be undermined.

AVOID TREATING A SIXTEEN-YEAR-OLD LIKE A SIX-YEAR-OLD
In closing, let me offer one more suggestion on the issue of avoiding provocation: allow authority and discipline gradually to give way to friendly persuasion. Now, at all times in the nurturing of a child these two elements should be present. As I've already suggested, there will be occasions, even when your child is at a very young age, when a word of advice will be sufficient discipline, but parents do well to bear in mind that a sixteen-year-old cannot be ruled like a six-year-old. Gradually, over the years, parents should be seeking to replace authority over their children with gentle persuasion or parental advice. This requires a great deal of wisdom; nevertheless, a time must come when parental authority must stop. Remember that parents ought to be preparing their children to stand on their own two feet and to make their own way in life. The parents who try to control the sixteen- or eighteen-year-old as they would the six- or eight-year-old will only succeed in provoking their child to anger,[16] and possibly even render them incapable of making educated or well-thought-through decisions for themselves. Children must be held accountable for their actions, and at the same time they need to be given the space to

develop and grow into responsible young adults.

These are only a few practical examples of how a child can become exasperated and lose heart; I'm sure that any parents reading this book will be able to give many more examples. But remember, don't expect more from your child than he or she is capable of doing. Don't try to put an 'old head on young shoulders'. Allow children the opportunity to be children; allow them to fail and make mistakes, without giving them the sledgehammer treatment. Learn to distinguish between a child's natural capacity to fail and open defiance, and treat each situation accordingly. Don't cause your children to lose heart; rather, bring them up 'in the discipline and instruction of the Lord'. Parents are to 'bring up' and 'train up' their children, not keep them dependent and infantile. Children in the process of maturity must be given more and more opportunities to take on responsibility, make decisions and express creativity.

Study questions

FOR DISCUSSION
1. Re-read the section 'Punishment as a form of discipline'.
   (a) Discuss biblical reasons why parents must be extremely careful in their use of 'the rod' as a means of disciplining their children.
   (b) In what ways can the use of 'the rod' in discipline be seen as an expression of love?
2. 'The rod' should never be the primary method of disciplining a child. Discuss this comment.
3. Re-read 'Encouragement as a form of discipline'. Discuss practical ways in which parents can encourage their children without sounding condescending.
4. How important is a godly example as a means of discipline? In what ways will you as a parent seek to set this example?
5. Read Ephesians 6:4.
   (a) How important do you consider 'instruction in the Lord' to be for your family?
   (b) Discuss ways in which you can make this possible in your home.

Chapter 9

6. Read Colossians 3:21.
   (a) How important is it to avoid constant criticism of your child?
   (b) Discuss each of the other 'Faults to avoid'.

FOR PERSONAL REFLECTION

7. As a parent, how do you think you measure up to God's standards for parenting?
8. What practical measures are you prepared to take to improve your parenting skills?

Notes

1 **John Calvin** on Psalm 127, *Commentaries*, vol. 6 (Grand Rapids: Baker Book House, 1998).

2 **Jerry Bridges,** *Trusting God Even When Life Hurts* (NavPress, 1988) is an excellent book on the theme of understanding God's sovereignty when we face difficulties.

3 See **Rienecker,** *Linguistic Key to the Greek New Testament* (Grand Rapids: Zondervan, 1976), p. 540 on this verse.

4 παιδείᾳ

5 **Joseph H. Thayer,** *Thayer's Greek-English Lexicon of the New Testament* (Grand Rapids: Baker Book House, 1977), p. 473.

6 **Rienecker,** p. 504.

7 See 2 Samuel 15 on King David's troubled relationship with his son Absalom.

8 νουθεσία, with the basic meaning of 'instruction' or 'warning'.

9 **Palmer,** *The Family*, p. 82.

10 **James,** *A Help to Domestic Happiness,* p. 132.

11 **John Calvin,** *Commentaries*, vol. 21 (Ephesians) (Grand Rapids: Baker Book House, 1998), p. 328.

12 Ibid.

13 **Palmer,** p. 91.

14 For an example of this in the Bible read about Joseph and his brothers in Genesis 37.

15 **Palmer,** p. 94.

16 Ibid. p. 95.

Communication in the home

Therefore, laying aside falsehood, speak truth, each one of you, with his neighbor, for we are members of one another. Be angry, and yet do not sin; do not let the sun go down on your anger, and do not give the devil an opportunity … Let no unwholesome word proceed from your mouth, but only such a word as is good for edification according to the need of the moment, that it may give grace to those who hear. And do not grieve the Holy Spirit of God, by whom you were sealed for the day of redemption. Let all bitterness and wrath and anger and clamor and slander be put away from you, along with all malice. And be kind to one another, tender-hearted, forgiving each other, just as God in Christ also has forgiven you (Ephesians 4:25–27, 29–32).

If looks could kill!
In a classic Irish film of 1990 called *The Field*, Richard Harris plays the role of 'Bull' McCabe. The film is set in rural Ireland in the 1930s and, as his name in the film suggests, 'Bull' McCabe is a rather formidable and headstrong character. One scene in the film depicts 'Bull', his wife Maggie (Brenda Fricker) and their son Tadgh (Sean Bean) all sitting down to supper. 'Bull' and Maggie haven't spoken for years and the atmosphere is rather tense, to say the least. Maggie places the food before 'Bull' and Tadgh without speaking a word and the meal is eaten in silence apart from the sounds of 'Bull' slurping his soup. The relationship between husband and wife is so strained that Tadgh, fed up with the whole affair, gets up from the table and leaves in disgust.

The scene is a classic example of the wrong sort of communication in the family. Although 'Bull' and Maggie had not spoken for years, they were nevertheless communicating very effectively. The looks across the table were as sharp as a knife and their body language 'spoke' volumes.

In this chapter I want to look at the importance of good communication in the family. In particular, I want to consider God's prescription for the right type of communication. To do this we will consider communication under three general headings: sending messages, receiving messages, and responding to messages. Before we look at these three areas of study, let me establish what I consider to be two fundamental elements in the art of good communication.

Firstly, good or effective communication is quite simply the passing on of information to another person in a way that ensures that the message is understood as it was intended. Now, if that was the only criterion for communication, we could justifiably say rather nasty and hurtful things to people who are upsetting or hurting us. However, God's prescription for good communication has another very important element. In Ephesians 4:29 we read these words: 'Let no unwholesome word proceed from your mouth, but only such a word as is good for edification according to the need of the moment, that it may give grace to those who hear.'

The apostle Paul here gives us what I consider to be the second fundamental element in good communication. According to God's Word, all communication should be to help others, not to hurt them. Speech is a wonderful gift from God, and of all the wonderful gifts that God has given us it is perhaps the most misused; I dare to suggest that we are all guilty in this area. Jesus also taught the importance of controlling our speech when he warned us that God will hold us accountable for every word we say. Is that not a very challenging thought? Yet how often we fail in this fundamental area of our Christian lives! 'Let no unwholesome word proceed from your mouth.' In other words, we are to say nothing that is hurtful, coarse or unhelpful, and instead say only that which is good for helping others.

With these fundamental principles in mind, let's move on to the first of our three general headings.

Sending messages

NON-VERBAL COMMUNICATION

As I have already hinted at in my illustration of 'Bull' McCabe and his wife, even where words are absent, communication still takes place. Communication is more than words: it also involves sending many non-verbal messages. There are many examples of this in the Bible, for example:

ADAM AND EVE

When Adam and Eve took and ate the forbidden fruit in Genesis 3. Without saying a word, they sent a very powerful message to God, in effect: 'We believe that in forbidding us to eat this fruit, you are keeping back something that is good for us and we want it.' In a sense they were saying that they trusted their own judgement more than God's. By reaching out and taking that fruit, Eve, without speaking a word, said very clearly, 'I don't believe you, God, when you say that I will die.' Her action showed a lack of trust in and respect for God.

ABRAHAM

Now the LORD appeared to him by the oaks of Mamre, while he was sitting at the tent door in the heat of the day. And when he lifted up his eyes and looked, behold, three men were standing opposite him; and when he saw them, he ran from the tent door to meet them, and bowed himself to the earth (Genesis 18:1–2).

The Hebrew word translated here as 'bowed down'[1] is the same word used in Exodus 34:14 (and many other places in Scripture) to signify bowing down to worship or to show respect. Abraham, by bowing down before these three men, was, without speaking a word, communicating his respect for them.

ISAAC

So Isaac lived in Gerar. When the men of the place asked about his wife, he said, 'She is my sister,' for he was afraid to say, 'my wife,' thinking, 'the men of the place might kill me on account of Rebekah, for she is beautiful.' And it came about, when he had been there a long time, that Abimelech king of the Philistines *looked out through a window, and saw*, and behold, Isaac was caressing his wife Rebekah. Then Abimelech called Isaac and said, 'Behold, certainly she is your wife! How then did you say, "She is my sister"?' And Isaac said to him, 'Because I said, "Lest I die on account of her"' (Genesis 26:6–9, emphasis mine).

Here we have a wonderful example of how actions can speak louder than words. Although Isaac said that Rebekah was his sister, when Abimelech looked out of his window he saw not the sort of behaviour that happens between a brother and sister, but a man expressing his tender affection for his wife. Isaac, by his behaviour towards Rebekah, communicated very clearly to Abimelech that she was in fact his wife. Without speaking a word, Isaac was communicating his love for Rebekah.

Let's consider one final example of non-verbal communication, this time from the New Testament.

WITNESSES OF THE CRUCIFIXION
And Jesus, crying out with a loud voice, said, 'Father, into Thy hands I commit My spirit.' And having said this, He breathed His last. Now when the centurion saw what had happened, he began praising God, saying, 'Certainly this man was innocent.' And all the multitudes who came together for this spectacle, when they observed what had happened, began to return, beating their breasts (Luke 23:46–48).

The scene is of Jesus speaking his last words on the cross. As he breathed his last breath, the people who had come to witness this spectacle turned to go home. We read that, as they went, they beat their breasts. In Bible times, beating one's breast in this manner was a very expressive gesture. William Hendriksen refers to the scene like this: 'So, returning to the city, they began to *beat their breasts in self-reproach*' (emphasis mine).[2] Thayer's study on the Greek text says that to beat one's own breast was a sign of a wounded or disquieted conscience.[3] The non-verbal communication is very powerful. These people, who had come to witness a man being wounded to the point of death, walked away in silence, beating their breasts as a sign of their own wounded consciences. Without speaking a word, they communicated very clearly their own guilt.

These are only a few of the many examples in the Bible of non-verbal communication, but I hope that they are sufficient to express just how powerful non-verbal communication can be. By their behaviour, Adam and Eve expressed their lack of trust and respect for God, whereas Abraham expressed profound respect for his three visitors. Isaac expressed his love for Rebekah, and the witnesses to the crucifixion expressed a guilty conscience. All of this communication took place without one word being spoken.

There are many ways in which we communicate with our families without speaking a word:

OUR EYES

We communicate our attitudes by the manner in which we look or don't look at someone.[4] For example, if someone is listening to you with his or her eyes open really wide, it can indicate a sense of disbelief in the sense of 'Do you really mean that?' or 'Did you really say that just now?' If I roll my eyes, it can communicate my displeasure at what I am hearing, or perhaps even indicate that I have heard something similar before, saying, 'Oh no, not again!' By rolling my eyes I may even be displaying scorn at what I have just heard or seen. Specialists suggest that, very often, when people are lying they tend to look down. If my eyes are looking all around the room while you are talking to me, it can indicate that I'm not very interested in what you have to say.

Augustine touched on another area in which a lot can be communicated with our eyes. In a letter to the nuns at his sister's monastery he said, 'For it is not only by touch that a woman awakens in any man or cherishes towards him such desire, this may be done by inward feelings and by looks.'[5]

The principle is particularly relevant in our day for those who are married. If a husband or wife is exchanging glances with a member of the opposite sex, he or she is in danger of unfaithfulness to the marriage partner. As Augustine puts it, 'though the tongue is silent ... their purity of character is gone, though their bodies are not defiled by any act of uncleanness.'[6]

OUR FACIAL EXPRESSIONS

Facial expressions can be very powerful ways of communicating our inner feelings, for example, happiness, sadness, anger, etc. Proverbs 15:13 says, 'A joyful heart makes a cheerful face.'

OUR HANDS

If we place a hand gently on someone's shoulder when that person is sad or distressed, we are expressing sympathy with him or her. By holding up an open hand, palm outwards, we are saying that we want the other person to stop talking, In Albanian culture, by moving an open hand in a slightly chopping movement we are saying, 'I'm going to discipline you.'

OUR LISTENING

By listening carefully, or not listening carefully, to someone, we communicate whether we are interested or not in what he or she is saying.

OUR POSTURE AND BEHAVIOUR

We send messages by the way we sit or stand, or by the way we use our time. Folding of arms during a conversation may indicate lack of agreement or even a retreat into a defensive position. The amount of time we give to a project is very often a reflection of how important that project is to us.

The point I am making is that there are many forms of non-verbal communication. Our actions, our manner and our attitudes, in fact, our whole demeanour, affect how we communicate with others.

There is a problem, however, with non-verbal communication. The problem is that it can be very easily misread or misunderstood. The story of Hannah is a good example of this. In 1 Samuel 1:12–15 we read the following:

Now it came about, as she continued praying before the LORD, that Eli was watching her mouth. As for Hannah, she was speaking in her heart, only her lips were moving, but her voice was not heard. So Eli thought she was drunk. Then Eli said to her, 'How long will you make yourself drunk? Put away your wine from you.' But Hannah answered and said, 'No, my lord, I am a woman oppressed in spirit; I have drunk neither wine nor strong drink, but I have poured out my soul before the LORD.'

Hannah was in the temple, praying that God would give her a son. She was pouring her heart out before God, and was so focused upon her appeal to him that she did not realize that Eli was beside her.

I have to say that I wish more Christians were like Hannah. If only more Christians were as serious about prayer, and so fervent in their praying that they could just ignore the distractions around them, it would indeed be a tremendous blessing to the church. How many of us are easily distracted when we ought to be praying, when we ought to be giving God our undivided attention? Not Hannah. She was so focused upon pouring her heart out to God that 'only her lips were moving, but her voice was not heard' (v. 13).

Hannah was not like the Pharisees, who loved to be heard by men. She was in deep and earnest prayer, but her sincerity with God was misunderstood. Eli, seeing her lips moving but hearing no sound, 'thought that she was drunk'! He misunderstood Hannah's behaviour and her non-verbal communication. This shows us that our non-verbal communication can be misunderstood by others. We must realize that our wives, husbands, friends or families may misunderstand our behaviour. They may very easily misunderstand why we are in a quiet mood, why we have a frown upon our face or why we look at them in a particular way. There are two very simple points to make here. Firstly, we should do everything we can to ensure that others do not misunderstand us. Secondly, if we have no good reason to do otherwise, we should always interpret the actions of others (their non-verbal communications) in a positive light: 'Love is patient... bears all things, believes all things, hopes all things, endures all things' (1 Corinthians 13:4, 7).

I remember vividly an incident during my teaching practice in a school in Cambridge. I was observing my tutor teach a class and, to my bewilderment, she became very defensive towards me, even a little angry. For some time I genuinely did not understand what the problem was. In the end it turned out to be very simple. As she was teaching, my tutor thought that I was looking at her with disapproval. In other words, she thought that I was finding fault with her teaching methods.

In actual fact, I was enjoying her lesson and was really concentrating hard upon what she was saying and doing, but obviously something about me was sending out the wrong signals. Somehow I was giving her the wrong impression. From that incident I have come to realize that when I am really concentrating or listening intently to someone, I have a very stern look upon my face; my tutor had interpreted that 'stern' look as being one of disapproval. It was a valuable lesson to learn. I now know that, when I am listening intently to someone, I need to smile occasionally so that they may be encouraged and not misunderstand me.

The point is that we all need to be very careful with the non-verbal messages we send out and, whenever possible, we should help others to understand us properly. The following extract from Wayne Mack is insightful: 'Non-verbal communication is continuous, powerful, and easily misunderstood … [Therefore] we must work at carefully sending and receiving non-verbal messages. Families are often devastated by failure in this aspect of their relationships. Don't let it happen to you.'[7]

VERBAL COMMUNICATION

So we have seen how easily non-verbal communication can be misunderstood. Many disagreements in the home (and, indeed, in the church and society) result from this problem. Since non-verbal communication can be so easily misunderstood, isn't it wonderful that we have the gift of speech?

Unfortunately, things are never quite that simple. In James 3:8–9 we read, 'But no one can tame the tongue; it is a restless evil and full of deadly poison. With it we bless our Lord and Father; and with it we curse men, who have been made in the likeness of God.'

Speech is, without doubt, a wonderful gift from God, but how effective are we at using it in the way that God intended? Speech, when used properly, can promote understanding and agreement, and can be a wonderful means of encouraging others,[8] but when used badly or misused, speech can hurt and offend, and seriously damage relationships. There are three basic dangers in our use of speech.

THE DANGER OF NOT ENOUGH WORDS

The story is told of a man who bought a parrot that spoke five languages. Having made his purchase, the new owner was assured by the seller that the parrot would be delivered to his home after two hours. Content with his purchase, the man went to work, and during the day he told all his workmates about this wonderful multilingual parrot that he had bought. After work he went straight home and excitedly asked his wife if the parrot had arrived.

'Yes,' replied his wife.

'Where is it?' he asked impatiently.

'In the oven, baking, but it isn't ready yet,' replied his wife.

'In the oven?' exclaimed the man in desperation. 'But that parrot knew five languages!'

His wife calmly replied, 'Well, that's strange, because it hasn't opened its mouth yet!'[9]

Sometimes silence can be a dangerous thing. Perhaps if the parrot had spoken, the wife would have realized its worth. The book of Proverbs gives many indications that there are times when the wise thing is to remain silent. Ecclesiastes 3:7 also makes this point: there we are reminded that there is a time to be silent, but that there is also a time to speak. Many families are only held together because the wife refuses to confront her husband with his faults. Every time he says or does something to hurt her, for the sake of peace she just keeps it all inside. This was never how God intended a relationship between husband and wife to be; a relationship where one person is afraid to share his or her concerns with the other is surely in danger of being as dead as the parrot in the oven. As I pointed out in a previous study, love does not forbid it but actually demands that couples should point out each other's faults (see Matthew 5:21–25 and 18:15–16).

Let me hasten to add that confrontation for the sake of confrontation is not right, either. Often resentment is allowed to build up to the point of explosion and words are then used as weapons that can wound. Nevertheless, while taking every precaution to avoid this wrong use of language or this wrong approach to dealing with difficulties within the family, husband and wife should help each other by pointing out each other's faults. This, according to Scripture, should be done with tenderness and love. Paul makes this point in Ephesians 4:15 when he says that we must 'speak the truth in love'. Beware of the danger of silence in your relationship.

There is also a danger in speaking and in not saying quite enough for your partner to understand you clearly. John Gray, in his book *Men are from Mars, Women are from Venus*, draws attention to the different vocabulary that men and women use. He suggests that women very often drop hints rather than say exactly what they want. For example, when a wife says, 'We never go out', the husband might respond by saying, 'That's not true. We went out last week.'[10] He has missed the point completely. You see, when the wife says, 'We never go out', what she really means is, 'I would really like to do something together. What do you think? Will you take me out tonight?' It's obvious, isn't it?

I would not dispute John Gray's point that husbands need to pay very close attention to their wives, but there is another very important biblical principle that, when applied, can resolve any ambiguities. In James 4:2 we read, 'You do not have because you do not ask.' The point that James is making is that there are many quarrels and unnecessary disappointments because people do not pray, they do not ask, they do not make their requests known to God. There is nobody who knows our minds better than God. He knows our every thought. He knows our needs before we speak, and yet he reminds us through James that we do not have because we do not ask. We do not consult with God as to whether something is best for us or not, and because we do not make our requests known to God, or because we ask for the wrong reasons or in the wrong way, we face continual disappointment. The principle I want to draw out of this verse is very simple: Good communication comes as the result of speaking clearly, in the right manner and with the right motives, not by dropping hints. Some suggest that, because life is so complicated, it is perhaps more realistic to suggest that we ought to learn to read between the lines. I want to suggest exactly the opposite. Because life is so complicated, we ought rather to learn to express ourselves as clearly as possible. We have already seen that non-verbal communication is open to serious misunderstanding. The same danger is present when we do speak but fail to do so in a clear way or to say enough. Beware of the danger of not enough words. On the other hand, beware of the danger of too many words.

During my time in Bible college, my friends and I very often had theological debates. Despite the fact that we were very good friends, sometimes the debates became quite intense. In his attempt to win a debate, one friend very often employed the technique of talking non-stop. To make sure that his point was understood he would talk and talk and, even after he had made his point very clearly indeed, he would continue to talk. You see, so long as he kept talking, no one could reply to his claims or attempt to prove him wrong.

How many disputes in the home are 'won' by one person 'rattling on' and not taking time to listen to what the others have to say? This was essentially the method used by the Ephesians, of whom we read in Acts 19:34. On that occasion they continued to shout for two hours so that Alexander could not make his defence.

We would do well to remember God's Word on this subject: 'When there are many words, transgression is unavoidable, but he who restrains his lips is wise' (Proverbs 10:19). There is often much wisdom in saying little. Now, the problem, or the sin, is not that a person may say a lot. Sometimes we need to use many words to make a point clearly. The problem is that those who speak a lot do not always take time to think a lot about the words that they are using. As a result, they may say things that are unnecessary, improper, inaccurate or even offensive. People use words carelessly and can often do more harm than good. It is a wise person indeed who chooses his or her words carefully and avoids saying too much.

Beware of the danger of not enough words. Likewise, beware of the danger of too many words. Thirdly, we need to beware of using misleading words.

THE DANGER OF USING MISLEADING WORDS

What do I mean by 'misleading' words? Well, the most obvious form is blatant lying. There are, of course, many warnings in Scripture against lying, and most people are aware of how serious and wrong it is. But I want to draw your attention to a few more subtle forms of lying.

Half-truths: In Genesis 20:1–12 we find an example of how half-truths are often used to cover up the whole truth:

Chapter 10

Now Abraham journeyed from there toward the land of the Negev, and settled between Kadesh and Shur; then he sojourned in Gerar. And Abraham said of Sarah his wife, 'She is my sister.' So Abimelech king of Gerar sent and took Sarah. But God came to Abimelech in a dream of the night, and said to him, 'Behold, you are a dead man because of the woman whom you have taken, for she is married.' Now Abimelech had not come near her; and he said, 'Lord, will You slay a nation, even though blameless? Did he not himself say to me, "She is my sister"? And she herself said, "He is my brother." In the integrity of my heart and the innocence of my hands I have done this.' Then God said to him in the dream, 'Yes, I know that in the integrity of your heart you have done this, and I also kept you from sinning against Me; therefore I did not let you touch her. Now therefore, restore the man's wife, for he is a prophet, and he will pray for you, and you will live. But if you do not restore her, know that you shall surely die, you and all who are yours.'

So Abimelech arose early in the morning and called all his servants and told all these things in their hearing; and the men were greatly frightened. Then Abimelech called Abraham and said to him, 'What have you done to us? And how have I sinned against you, that you have brought on me and on my kingdom a great sin? You have done to me things that ought not to be done.' And Abimelech said to Abraham, 'What have you encountered, that you have done this thing?' And Abraham said, 'Because I thought, surely there is no fear of God in this place; and they will kill me because of my wife. Besides, she actually is my sister, the daughter of my father, but not the daughter of my mother, and she became my wife.'

This is the second of two occasions when Abraham tried to protect himself by pretending that Sarah, his wife, was actually his sister. In fact, what he said was partly true. As verse 12 points out, Sarah was in fact Abraham's half-sister. So the sin was not so much in what he said, but in what he did not say. Now, I'm not suggesting that we go around wearing our hearts on our sleeves or that we should always tell everyone all our private affairs. We have already considered the danger of too many words. Abraham's fault or sin lay not in the fact that he did not tell Abimelech all his private or family affairs, but in the fact that he told a half-truth with the clear purpose of deceiving. In doing this he not only lied, but also showed a lack of trust in God. I particularly like John Calvin's challenge on this very point. He says,

'If we thoroughly examine ourselves, scarcely anyone will be found who will not acknowledge that he has often offended in the same way.'[11]

It's an absolute tragedy that God's people often respond to difficulties or danger by using deception and that they do so with a clear conscience![12] Abraham had satisfied his own conscience by knowing that Sarah was indeed his half-sister. In a similar fashion, we can satisfy our consciences by knowing that what we have said was indeed half-true. But beware of the sin of deception! It is better by far to tell the whole truth and trust in God for the consequences. Beware of telling half-truths.

Exaggeration:[13] Sometimes we exaggerate about others. How often have husbands or wives spoken to each other like this: 'You're *always* late', 'You shout *all* the time' or 'You have an excuse for *everything*'? Sometimes we exaggerate about ourselves. We might say, 'I *never* do that', 'I'm *always* ready on time' or 'I'm *dying*' (i.e. tired). Now the danger with exaggeration of this nature is that, after a while, people simply stop listening to it, or worse, it causes others to disbelieve what you say.

Misrepresentation: This is a more sinister form of exaggeration. We misrepresent others by taking their words or actions out of context, and twist the truth by adding to it or taking away from it. Often people (sadly even Christians) will do this in an attempt to make their own case stronger. It is also a favourite weapon in the arsenal of husbands and wives. In an attempt to avoid actually facing up to their own faults, disagreeing couples will often seek to draw the attention away from themselves by misrepresenting what the other partner actually said or did. This often occurs when one partner shares with a friend some of the difficulties within the marriage. To make his or her own case more plausible the faults of the partner are exaggerated. A serious side effect of this type of misrepresentation is that those who have been misrepresented often tend to stop talking about important issues because they fear being misquoted again. As a result, such a person will ensure that the topic of conversation at any given time remains very light and superficial. It is obvious that this is not the sort of communication likely to help develop a healthy marriage relationship.

These are just a few of the ways in which relationships in the family, church and society can be seriously damaged, but they are surely a warning to us of the importance of good communication, that is, communication as God intended it to be. Build up confidence in others by clear, unambiguous and gracious words: 'Let your speech always be with grace, seasoned, as it were, with salt, so that you may know how you should respond to each person' (Colossians 4:6). In layman's terms, speak in such a way that others want to listen, and listen in such a way that others want to speak.

Receiving messages

HEAR WHAT IS BEING SAID

You would think that receiving verbal messages should be a relatively simple matter. After all, it is just a matter of listening. Yet so many relationships are damaged precisely because people do not hear what is being said.

In James 1:19 we read, 'This you know, my beloved brethren. But let everyone be quick to hear, slow to speak and slow to anger.' Be quick to listen and slow to speak ... but most people do just the opposite. They are quick to speak and do not take the time to listen carefully to what the other person has to say. Good listening is a discipline that needs to be cultivated and demands some hard work. Unfortunately, many people never take the time to cultivate this important element of good communication. As a result, what often happens is that, when something important needs to be discussed within a family, or simply between a husband and wife, you find two parties talking *at* each other rather than talking *to* each other. When this happens, most of the essential talk is lost because neither party is taking the time to listen properly to the other. In many situations you find two people talking at the same time, or at least constantly interrupting the other before he or she has finished speaking.

Just think about some of the conversations that you have had recently, and try to count the number of times when one person interrupted the other. Of course, one may interrupt another with the genuine purpose of seeking to clarify what is being said. Seeking clarity is obviously a positive element in good communication, but I would still suggest that such clarity should be sought after the other person has finished speaking. Sadly (and I am hazarding a guess at this point since I do not have any scholarly opinion to support me), it would appear that most interruptions are not actually necessary, and may well simply be a sign that the person interrupting is not really listening properly. How can one be truly listening and genuinely trying to understand the other person if he or she is constantly breaking the flow of thought by interrupting? How can you be listening well if you are talking?

Neither can you listen if you are thinking about the next thing that you want to say. Even if you keep your thoughts on a conversation, you will never hear properly if you are rehearsing what you will say next. Discipline yourself to listen properly. Quiet, patient listening is indispensable if two people are going to understand each other. Good listening will help you gather more complete and accurate information, and this will help you to understand any potential problems. Try to develop the art of good listening. Try not to interrupt the other person, and try to keep your mind on what is being said rather than on what you want to say next. Hear what is being said.

HEAR ONLY WHAT IS BEING SAID

I have to confess that I have been neither gifted nor groomed in the art of public speaking. Even in private conversation I often fumble for words where others seem to flow so eloquently in what they are saying. This faltering style of speaking, especially when I am talking Albanian, has often led others to begin suggesting the word they think I am about to say. I can say that, to date, rarely has the other person suggested the correct word. For them to do so consistently would involve some degree of mind-reading. While it is true that we may occasionally make an accurate guess at what someone else is thinking, God has not given us a sixth sense of mind-reading. This being so, it is all the more important that we really do listen to hear exactly what other people are saying, and to hear only what they are saying.

A further development of this sort of mind-reading is the enjoyment many people seem to take trying to 'read between the lines'. In other words, they look for the supposedly hidden message behind the words the speaker is actually using. In Genesis 37 we read the story of how Joseph was despised by his older brothers, and how they eventually sold him into slavery. Many years later Joseph and his brothers were reunited in Egypt. By then Joseph had risen to a prominent position of leadership and controlled the food stores of all the land, and, because of the famine, his brothers were forced to go to Egypt to buy grain from him. We pick up the story in Genesis 50:15, some years after Joseph's entire family moved to live near him in Egypt and immediately after the death of his father:

When Joseph's brothers saw that their father was dead, they said, 'What if Joseph should bear a grudge against us and pay us back in full for all the wrong which we did to him!' So they sent a message to Joseph, saying, 'Your father charged before he died, saying, "Thus you shall say to Joseph, 'Please forgive, I beg you, the transgression of your brothers and their sin, for they did you wrong.'" And now, please forgive the transgression of the servants of the God of your father.' And Joseph wept when they spoke to him. Then his brothers also came and fell down before him and said, 'Behold, we are your servants.' But Joseph said to them, 'Do not be afraid, for am I in God's place? And as for you, you meant evil against me, but God meant it for good in order to bring about this present result, to preserve many people alive. So therefore, do not be afraid; I will provide for you and your little ones.' So he comforted them and spoke kindly to them (Genesis 50:15–21).

Here we have an excellent example of 'reading between the lines', of how people often pre-empt what another is going to say or do. Joseph's brothers had obviously thought long and hard about the situation, and had come to the conclusion that now their father was dead, Joseph would pay them back for the wrong that they had done. 'What if Joseph should bear a grudge?' they reasoned. Now, the sensible thing to have done would have been to go and talk to Joseph, and hear what he had to say before coming to any conclusions. However, they didn't. Instead, they decided that they knew Joseph's mind better than he knew it himself and jumped to the wrong conclusion.

This sort of thing happens in family life all the time. How many wives have hidden things from their husband because they think that he will disapprove or get angry? How many young people have said, 'There's no point asking Dad. He'll only say "No", anyway.' Communication often breaks down in families because one party pre-empts the response of the other, and therefore doesn't mention a particular matter at all. When receiving messages, hear what is being said and hear only what is being said. Be careful not to read more into a person's words or actions than is actually there. Be careful not to jump to conclusions. As Proverbs 18:13 says, 'He who gives an answer before he hears, it is folly and shame to him.'

That brings us to how we should respond to messages, for which I want to suggest four biblical principles.

Responding to messages

RESPOND POSITIVELY

Love ... bears all things, believes all things, hopes all things, endures all things (1 Corinthians 13:7).

In saying that love always believes and hopes, Paul is not suggesting that we should be naïve and blindly accept all things (i.e. the words and actions of others) without question. He is not saying that love always believes the best about everyone and everything,[14] rather that love never loses hope. There will be occasions when a person's words or actions will clearly show him or her to be untrustworthy, but unless we have a clear reason to do otherwise, we should interpret the actions or words of others in a positive manner.

RESPOND THOUGHTFULLY

The heart of the righteous ponders how to answer, but the mouth of the wicked pours out evil things (Proverbs 15:28).

On a number of occasions I have received a letter that has upset me, or someone has said something to upset me, and I think it is fair to say that we all have a tendency on such occasions to want to reply quickly so as to 'silence the ignorance of foolish men' (1 Peter 2:15). However, a hasty reply can often prove *you* to be the fool. God says we should ponder, meditate or study before answering a matter. Taking time to ponder a matter not only helps us to find the appropriate words with which to answer, it also gives time for our temper to cool so that we can reply in the appropriate attitude or manner—which brings me to our next point.

RESPOND GENTLY

A gentle answer turns away wrath, but a harsh word stirs up anger (Proverbs 15:1).

When responding, even to difficult situations, remember that a gentle answer turns away wrath. Even when the other person is in a rage, we should try to respond to that anger with a soft voice and a gentle manner. Matthew Henry says, 'Solomon, as conservator of the public peace, tells us how the peace must be kept … it is by soft words.'[15]

However, it is not enough just to be gentle and to use soft words; we must also …

RESPOND WITH HEALING WORDS

There is one who speaks rashly like the thrusts of a sword, but the tongue of the wise brings healing (Proverbs 12:18).

Some people have great control over their emotions and can remain calm even in the most difficult situations, yet at the same time they have a wonderful knack of knowing how to say exactly the right thing to infuriate and inflame an opponent. In fact, some people take great delight in stirring up others and watching them seethe with anger or frustration. Proverbs 12:18 commands against such behaviour. 'The tongue of the wise brings healing.' As Christians we are without excuse if we say (or do) something that will make a situation worse, and nowhere is that principle more important than in the family context, where each member knows so well the little things that irritate or upset the others. It is true, of course, that we may do or say something that will make a situation worse simply by telling the truth, or because what we have said is not well received despite our best intentions. I am no great believer in sacrificing truth for a quiet life, yet at all times the truth we speak must of necessity be tempered with genuine love and a sincere desire for reconciliation. At no time is it acceptable behaviour for a Christian to use even the truth merely as a weapon to inflict further wounds on any opponent.

This study has only scratched the surface of the important subject of good communication in the family. Good communication is essential for the development of a healthy family, and we would all do well to develop our communication skills.

In the words of Dr Jay Adams, 'Communication is fundamental to a Christ-centred home because it is the means by which a husband–wife relationship and parent–child relationship is established, grows, and is maintained.'[16]

Study questions

FOR DISCUSSION
1. Read Ephesians 4:25–27.
   (a) Discuss the principle for good communication found in this passage.
   (b) Give a brief definition of good communication.
2. In what ways do we often use non-verbal communication in the home?
3. What are the main dangers of non-verbal communication?
4. What difficulties might arise if:
   (a) We do not use enough words to explain ourselves?
   (b) We say too much?
5. Read Genesis 20:1–12.
   (a) In telling a half-truth, what exactly was Abraham's sin?
   (b) Using other words, how would you define a half-truth?
6. Discuss the dangers of exaggeration and misrepresentation.
7. Read James 1:19.
   (a) Why is it so important to be good listeners?
   (b) What are the dangers of 'reading between the lines' when someone speaks?
8. In what ways can we develop the art of responding positively to others?
9. What is a fundamental prerequisite to responding thoughtfully to others?
10. How important do you consider it to be to respond gently to others?

Chapter 10

FOR PERSONAL REFLECTION

11. How good are your communication skills? In what ways can you work to improve your communication skills with the rest of your family?

Notes

1 שחה shachah. This has the basic meaning 'to bow down', sometimes in homage before a superior or in worship before God.

2 **William Hendriksen,** *New Testament Commentary: The Gospel of Luke* (Grand Rapids: Baker Book House, 1978), p. 1037.

3 **Joseph H. Thayer,** *Thayer's Greek-English Lexicon of the New Testament* (Grand Rapids: Baker Book House, 1977), p. 632; Strong's Number 5180.

4 See **Mack,** *Your Family God's Way,* pp. 57ff for an excellent insight into non-verbal communication.

5 For full quote see Chapter 4 under 'Flee fornication'.

6 Ibid.

7 **Mack,** p. 64.

8 See **Ken Sande,** *The Peace Maker* (Grand Rapids: Baker Book House, 1991), p. 127.

9 **Isa Zymberi,** *Colloquial Albanian* (Routledge, 1991), p. 160.

10 **John Gray,** *Men are from Mars, Women are from Venus* (Thorsons, 1992), p. 60.

11 **John Calvin,** *Commentaries,* vol. 1 (Grand Rapids: Baker Book House, 1998), p. 521.

12 See also **Allen P. Ross,** *Creation and Blessing: A Guide to the Study and Exposition of Genesis* (Grand Rapids: Baker, 1988), p. 274.

13 See **Mack,** p. 117.

14 See **Gordon D. Fee,** *The First Epistle to the Corinthians,* NICNT (Grand Rapids: Eerdmans, 1987), p. 640.

15 **Matthew Henry,** *Commentary on the Whole Bible,* vol. 3 (Macdonald Publishing Company, n. d.), p. 873.

16 **Adams,** *Christian Living in the Home,* p. 28.

Preparing your family for eternity

And, fathers, do not provoke your children to anger; but bring them up in the discipline and instruction of the Lord (Ephesians 6:4).

There's simply not enough time!

Speaking in 1847, James W. Alexander, the pastor of a church in New York, said these words: 'In a period when the world is every day making inroads on the church, it has especially invaded the household … Along with Sabbath observance [i.e. keeping the Lord's Day special] family worship has lost ground.'[1]

If James Alexander could say these things about the demise of family worship more than a century and a half ago, I wonder what he would say today. Many things influence the young—their friends (peer pressure), school, television, etc.—but nothing has more influence upon a young person than the atmosphere and activities within his or her family. As believers in Christ we are all members of the universal family of God, and as such we are encouraged to meet regularly as a church for the reading of God's Word and prayer. During these times we pray for one another, as the Scriptures exhort us to do. But each nuclear family unit has its own particular needs, its own particular sorrows and dangers and its own particular problems, some of which they will not want to share with the wider Christian community. This is very natural and to be expected and respected. However, such needs, sorrows, dangers and problems still need to be addressed and laid before the Lord.

In seeking to address such private issues every individual within a family ought to be encouraged to have a personal quiet time with God; the reality is, however, that until children come to know the Lord personally, it is highly unlikely that they will have any desire to read their Bible or pray. Therefore the onus is upon Christian parents. Paul, in his instructions to

Christian parents, tells them to instruct their children in the things of God (Ephesians 6:4). Holloman writes, 'The family was utilized virtually from the beginning for spiritual purposes. It continues as the primary social context for teaching and modelling biblical truth to promote spiritual nurture.'[2] I agree wholeheartedly with these sentiments, however I fear that in many cases the family unit is not the primary context for spiritual nurture, as it ought to be. Many parents seem content, at best, to delegate this responsibility to the local church or Sunday school or, at worst, to ignore the need altogether.

In our day I believe that what may have started out as a healthy reaction to legalism, or a legalistic application of Scripture, has developed into an unhealthy overreaction. This can be seen in the tendency, noted above by Alexander, to move away from what he calls 'family worship'. Many see it as just 'too legalistic' to say that we ought to have a regular (perhaps even daily) time when the family gathers together for instruction from God's Word. Then, of course, there is the practical consideration that in homes where perhaps both parents work, it is extremely difficult to find a time that suits every member of the family. In the mornings there is a constant dash to get to the bathroom first, and queues of impatient parents or siblings. Breakfast is a very rushed affair, if everyone does actually take time to eat at all. Evenings are just as difficult. There are friends to meet, meetings to attend, television programmes to be watched. Time seems just too scarce to be spending it on family worship. On the issue of how much television we watch, Groucho Marx once told how he found television to be educating: 'Every time somebody turns on the set, I go into another room and read a book.'[3] Perhaps we can all learn from his example and occasionally break away from our television sets, not to read any old book, but to read the Book. Christian parent, do you really believe that this world is transitory, that we are here only for a short time in comparison with where we will be for eternity? Parents spend so much time (not unwisely) preparing their children to cope in this world. They try to provide the best possible education so that they are well prepared for the future. There is simply not enough time to fit in family worship! In Mark 8:36 the Lord asks, 'For what does it profit a man to gain the whole world, and forfeit his soul?' In light of such a clear exhortation from our Lord himself, I ask you to reconsider whether it really is true that there simply isn't enough time! Is it not negligence if parents fail to do all they can to prepare their child for eternity?

Perhaps the term 'family worship' is not altogether helpful. It conjures up the idea of a miniature church service. Perhaps a better way of putting it is simply to talk of Bible instruction in the home. However it is phrased, there certainly seem to be enough biblical examples, besides Ephesians 6:4, to justify and even commend a regular time of learning from the Scriptures in the home.

Biblical commands for instructing children in the home

• Deuteronomy 6:1–7: 'Now this is the commandment, the statutes and the judgments which the Lord your God has commanded me to teach you, that you might do them in the land where you are going over to possess it, so that you and your son and your grandson might fear the Lord your God, to keep all His statutes and His commandments, which I command you, all the days of your life, and that your days may be prolonged. O Israel, you should listen and be careful to do it, that it may be well with you and that you may multiply greatly, just as the Lord, the God of your fathers, has promised you, in a land flowing with milk and honey. Hear, O Israel! The Lord is our God, the Lord is one! And you shall love the Lord your God with all your heart and with all your soul and with all your might. And these words, which I am commanding you today, shall be on your heart; and you shall teach them diligently to your sons and shall talk of them when you sit in your house and when you walk by the way and when you lie down and when you rise up.'
• Deuteronomy 11:18–19: 'You shall therefore impress these words of mine on your heart and on your soul; and you shall bind them as a sign on your hand, and they shall be as frontals on your forehead. And you shall teach them to your sons, talking of them when you sit in your house and when you walk along the road and when you lie down and when you rise up.'
• Psalm 78:4–7:
  We will not conceal them from their children,
  But tell to the generation to come the praises of the Lord,
  And His strength and His wondrous works that He has done.

For He established a testimony in Jacob,
And appointed a law in Israel,
Which He commanded our fathers,
That they should teach them to their children,
That the generation to come might know, even the children yet to be born,
That they may arise and tell them to their children,
That they should put their confidence in God,
And not forget the works of God,
But keep His commandments.

A way of life

Before we move on to the specific issue of Bible instruction in the home, it is important to place it in the context of spiritual nurture in the family in general. In Chapter 9 I quoted John Angell James, who pointed out so clearly that the first book a child reads, and continues to read throughout life, is his or her parents' behaviour. It is so important that parents not only teach their children the right thing to do but that they also show them by example. This is especially true in the context of spiritual growth. If a parent is spiritually stagnant, it is to be expected that the child's spiritual growth will be affected. This very naturally leads me to the words of the Lord in Deuteronomy 6 quoted above: 'Now this is the commandment, the statutes and the judgments which the LORD your God has commanded me to teach you, that you might do them… (vv. 1ff).

Before parents can expect to teach their children biblical truth properly they ought first of all to be people who are serious about the religion they profess to believe. Children will very quickly see through any hypocrisy. Moses, in Deuteronomy 6, teaches the children of Israel the basics of what they are to do and why—'that you might do them' (v. 1). This is emphasized again in verse 3: 'You should listen and be careful to do it …' Many Christians seem to have a subtle leaning towards believing that, if they have some biblical knowledge stored up in some computerized device (such as the latest palm-top computer, for example) or in their minds, that is a sign of Christian growth or maturity. This sort of thinking is very far removed from the Hebrew idea.[4] For the Hebrew, it was foolishness to think of separating religious knowledge from conduct. The whole purpose of knowledge is so that conduct might change for the better. That is why in Deuteronomy 6:1 Moses emphasizes both 'hear' and 'do'.

Moses goes on in verse 7 to say, 'You shall *teach* them diligently to your sons and shall *talk* of them when you *sit* in your house and when you *walk* by the way and when you *lie* down and when you *rise* up' (emphasis added). The general idea behind this verse is that religious instruction in the family should be a way of life. It should be part of the natural activity of every day. Parents ought to cultivate the skill of teaching their children a biblical worldview. Children can be taught to appreciate God the creator in the beauties of nature as you 'walk by the way'. They can be taught basic biblical truths as you 'sit in your house', including the spiritual benefits of simply leaving our fears and concerns with God through prayer. As children lie down to sleep and rise up to a new day, they can be encouraged to talk to God to give him thanks for his daily provision, including a good night's rest. In other words, although a more formal time of Bible instruction certainly has its own value, children can be taught from an early age to appreciate God in the ordinary activities that take place in any home during the day. The worship of God ought to be a way of life, not simply an appendix to the day's activities.

Scriptural examples of biblical instruction in the home

Abraham is the first example we turn to. In Genesis 18 the Lord talks of Abraham as the one whom he has chosen to be a blessing for the world.[5] In verse 19 we read, 'For I have chosen him, in order that he may command his children and his household after him to keep the way of the LORD by doing righteousness and justice; in order that the LORD may bring upon Abraham what He has spoken about him.'

Here we find that Abraham had a specific duty towards his family. He was to teach, or command, his family to keep the way of the Lord. In other words, he was to lead his family in biblical instruction.

The Passover meal also gives us several helpful hints in relation to biblical instruction in the family (Exodus 12:21–28). Firstly, it teaches that the Passover meal was a family ritual. It was not simply to be observed by God's people in a special gathering or as individuals, but was to be an integral part of family life. In verse 21 Moses says, 'Take for yourselves lambs according to your families ...' Secondly, the Passover was not to be forgotten or neglected. Rather, it was to be observed continually and regularly. In verse 24 we read, 'And you shall observe this event as an ordinance for you and your children forever.' Thirdly, the Passover was not to be simply an outward ritual to be completed as quickly as possible so that the Israelites could get on with their day's work; rather, it was to be explained and its significance taught clearly. Look at verses 26–27: 'And it will come about when your children will say to you, "What does this rite mean to you?" that you shall say, "It is a Passover sacrifice to the LORD who passed over the houses of the sons of Israel in Egypt when He smote the Egyptians, but spared our homes."'

In the same way, biblical instruction is not simply for special gatherings of God's people; it should be a family ritual. It should be observed continually and regularly. It should aim to attract each person's attention so that all can understand what it is they are reading, hearing and doing. Each person should use the intellectual faculties God has given, be they mighty or meagre.

Now, you may be thinking that these examples happened before the introduction of temple worship when the family setting was the only place to conduct worship. Therefore, let's take an example from later in the history of Israel.

In 2 Samuel 6:17–18, 20 we read:

So they brought in the ark of the LORD and set it in its place inside the tent which David had pitched for it; and David offered burnt offerings and peace offerings before the LORD. And when David had finished offering the burnt offering and the peace offering, he blessed the people in the name of the LORD of hosts ... But when David returned to bless his household, Michal the daughter of Saul came out to meet David and said, 'How the king of Israel distinguished himself today! He uncovered himself today in the eyes of his servants' maids as one of the foolish ones shamelessly uncovers himself!'

This passage brings out two simple points in relation to our subject. Firstly, we see very clearly that worship was a community practice (v. 18), but, secondly, this did not diminish the fact that worship was also conducted within the family. We read very clearly in verse 20 that, after his involvement in public worship, 'David returned to bless his household'. The word 'bless' here is taken from the Hebrew word *barak*,[6] meaning 'to kneel down', presumably in the presence of God. In this instance David returned to his home to kneel down and seek God's blessing upon his family.

These are only a few examples which indicate that biblical instruction was conducted in the home. It must be admitted that all except the example of Abraham are of very specific occasions of worship; the Passover, for example, was a yearly event and to be observed on a national scale. The instance in David's life was part of the euphoria surrounding the return of the Ark of the Covenant to Jerusalem. But add to these examples those of Daniel kneeling three times a day, praying and giving thanks to God (Daniel 6:10); our Lord instructing his disciples to pray daily for their needs (i.e. bread, Matthew 6:11); the Bereans searching the Scriptures daily (Acts 17:11); and Lois and Eunice influencing Timothy's spiritual development in a positive way (2 Timothy 1:5). Taken together, these give us a general picture of both individual times of prayer and corporate family times of biblical instruction within the home.

Practical suggestions for biblical instruction in the home

WHO SHOULD LEAD?

Of course, it is one thing to suggest that we ought to have a time of biblical instruction in the home, but if this is to be done, how should we approach it? How are Christian parents to bring their children up in the instruction of the Lord? The first thing I want to address is the issue of who should lead the activity. In order to answer that question let me remind you of some of the passages we have just read. In Genesis 18:19 it was Abraham, the head of the family, who was instructed to 'command his children and household' to keep the way of the Lord. In 2 Samuel 6 it was David, again as head of his family, who took the initiative to kneel before the Lord and seek God's blessing on his family. Who should lead the time of instruction? Well, I think that the biblical pattern points out very clearly that it should be the head of the family, which in many instances will be the husband or father. There will, of course, be exceptions to this in practice, just as there are exceptions in the Scriptures. We know, for example, that Timothy's grandmother Lois and his mother Eunice (2 Timothy 1:5) had a big influence upon his spiritual development, and Lydia (Acts 16:15) obviously had a very strong influence upon her household in the area of worship (in Lydia's case there is no mention of a husband). But where there is a husband or father present and he is a believer, then it is his responsibility to take the lead. There are some very practical reasons for this. A survey on church attendance might lead us to the conclusion that church and religion is mostly just for women and children; in many churches there are clearly more women than men. As a challenge to any Christian man reading this book, I want to say that if we do not want to give the world that impression, or if fathers do not want to give their sons that impression, then Christian husbands and fathers need to be reminded of their obligations in the areas of church attendance, and, more specifically, of instructing their children in the Lord. As James Alexander says, 'he cannot be reminded of them too often.'[7]

THE IMPORTANCE OF READING THE BIBLE

The next issue that I want to address is the content of family worship. I think it is fair to suggest that the first and indispensable part of family worship should be the reading of Scripture. If this one element is omitted, then any time spent together can scarcely be called worship. The reasons for this ought to be obvious: it is the Word of God that brings understanding, that has the potential to lead the unregenerate person to salvation in Christ; it is the Word of God that brings understanding to the believer and directs him or her in how to live in order to please God. In many Christian families there may be those who daily hear the Word of God being read but have no desire to read it for themselves. Those who have no other information regarding God's will than that which they hear read during family worship may, over a period of time, acquire not only the knowledge of saving faith but a large amount of Christian instruction.[8] For unsaved children it is obviously essential to focus frequently on passages that show them Christ as the only Saviour and their need to turn to him.

Sometimes it is argued that children may be too young for this. In response, I want to suggest that even very small children understand much more than we sometimes think. Certainly during those early years of development a young mind has a wonderful ability of soaking up information. The brain is developing and the neurons are 'networking' and increasing rapidly in the number of connections they are making with other neurons, fashioning 'the connections ... that endow us with an individual, unique brain'.[9] At such a stage in the development of any young mind, when it is soaking up information like a sponge soaking up water, what better to store up in those young minds than the Word of God?

THE IMPORTANCE OF PRAYER

The second indispensable element of family worship is prayer. Christian growth is a spiritual exercise, and therefore we need to ask for help through prayer. 'On the one hand every Christian is responsible to obey biblical truth. On the other hand they can and must depend on the Holy Spirit.'[10] It is the Holy Spirit that can transform Christians more and more into the likeness of Christ (Romans 8:2–17) and this life-transforming power is ours through prayer.

In 1647, the General Assembly of the Free Church of Scotland published a small *Directory for Family Worship* in which it was written, '... so many as can conceive prayer, ought to make use of that gift of God'.[11] The same document goes on to offer some practical guidelines for the contents of prayer. It says:

Let them confess to God how unworthy they are ... to confess their sins ... to pour out their souls to God for the forgiveness of sins. They are to give thanks to God for his many mercies especially for his love in Christ and the light of the gospel. They ought to pray for the whole church of Christ in general and the whole body of the congregation where they are members. The prayer may be closed with an earnest desire that God may be glorified in the coming kingdom of his Son.

Our prayers, then, should include at least the following elements:
- Praise to God for his greatness and his love, mercy and goodness to us; and for his plan of salvation and the giving of his only Son, the Lord Jesus Christ, to pay the price for our sin.
- Confession of our sins. We may not like to admit it but the Bible is clear that we are all guilty of sin (Romans 3:23) every day. Our sin may differ

from one person to the next and take many different forms: the wrong things we do, the wrong things we say, the wrong things we think, our failure to do the things we know we ought to do. When confessing our sins it is good to include these basic elements and to teach our children the importance of our thoughts and motives as well as our actions and words.

- Prayer for other people. Parents should teach their children to pray for others at an early age, and thus cultivate an others-centric, as opposed to an egocentric, life. Teach your children to pray for missionaries who are serving God in other parts of the world. A useful book to help with this is *Window on the World* by Daphne Spraggett and Jill Johnstone.[12]
- Thanks. This is a very important part of our prayers. How often we ask God for help but forget to thank him when he does help us! If children are to be encouraged to pray over their problems, then they should also be encouraged to say 'thank you' to God when he answers their prayers. This exercise has the added benefit of encouraging and developing faith in young hearts as children see God take a personal interest in them.

This is only a skeleton outline of ideas to be prayed for and can be adapted to suit particular situations. Allow me to add just one small element to that skeleton. It is good if your prayers include at least one small point taken from the Bible reading for that day. In other words, pray through at least one thing that you have read in the Bible on that occasion. If you do not clearly understand what you have just read or do not see how it applies to your life, then ask God to enlighten your understanding and to show you how it applies in your day-to-day chores. The Word of God contains wonderful promises, stern warnings and rebukes. It also contains wonderful encouragements, and we should incorporate all these elements into our daily prayer life. This could be viewed as a sort of watering of the seed of the Word of God with a refreshing shower of prayer and causing it to grow in our hearts and lives to the glory of God.

THE PLACE OF SINGING

Singing as part of worship is sanctioned by Scripture, as we are exhorted to sing psalms and hymns and spiritual songs (Ephesians 5:19; Colossians 3:16). Singing, especially with small children, is a very important part of worship. Young children love to sing and, of course, singing is a means of teaching biblical truth. Children will retain songs in their minds when perhaps they may not remember Bible passages. There are many Christian songs suitable for small children. Many have been produced by Child Evangelism Fellowship and can be purchased from them.[13]

THE PLACE OF MEMORIZATION

Teaching memory verses is also a very good way to instruct children and to help them retain the Word of God in their hearts and minds. I suggest that you keep passages short enough for your child to be encouraged with success in learning. In this way, longer passages can be taught over a period of time.

THE IMPORTANCE OF A REGULAR TIME

A practical help to sustaining Bible instruction in the home is to ensure that it happens at a regular fixed time each day. This way much procrastinating can be avoided, and everyone in the home will know what to expect. As to the amount of time to spend, let me offer the wise words of Alexander once again: 'something gentle, quiet and moderate should be our aim'.[14] In other words, the time should not be so long as to be a burden to the whole family or a bore to the younger children with their shorter concentration spans. At the same time, it should be long enough for family members to enter into meaningful dialogue with God. Any biblical instruction ought also to be conducted with a sense of reverence; yet that does not mean that it cannot be made fun, especially for the smaller children. There is nothing wrong with using a funny story to make a point (just as in preaching). If you are going to keep children and young people interested, then do all you can to avoid unnecessary gloom and cold formality. This does not mean you avoid challenging them of their very real need of Christ!

THE IMPORTANCE OF VARIETY

Variation each day will go a long way in avoiding such formality, and a family's changing needs will be a natural help in this. The person leading can also bring variety by suggesting different prayer requests and delegating the responsibilities of reading and prayer to various family members; not to mention keeping the whole exercise simple and interesting enough for the youngest in the family to understand. There are many books available today that explain the Bible in language that even a toddler can understand. Why not invest in your child's future by purchasing a number of these and using them for their instruction in righteousness?

These are only a few suggestions to get you thinking, and hopefully to get you motivated. The benefits of daily family worship are probably immeasurable, but allow me to offer a few encouragements, first of all for parents. The father or husband who will lead his family day by day, year after year, as the spiritual instructor and example to his family in worship will surely be affected personally and will, no doubt, grow deeper in his own relationship with God and knowledge of the Bible. The godly wife or mother may well find it easier to submit to the husband, whom she sees daily exhorting others and applying the Word of God to himself. The children will see that religion is a serious matter, and will have the Word of God planted in their hearts from an early age.

With the busyness of each day it is very easy to avoid spending time reading the Bible. Let me remind you that we are only here for a short time, seventy to eighty years on average, the Bible says. Just look around you and observe the effort that people are putting into preparing and working to make those seventy to eighty years as comfortable as possible. Yet the life to come is eternal. Should not that cause us to make even greater efforts to prepare for that life? By the faithful observance of biblical instruction in the home you will be employing a (daily?) means towards the salvation and sanctification of your family. If that is not enough to stir you up to its practice, surely the thought of the everlasting damnation of your children will cause you to use every means at your disposal to avoid such a catastrophe.[15]

Why not begin today to lay up treasures in heaven that can never be spoiled (Matthew 6:20)?

Study questions

FOR DISCUSSION

1. According to the section 'A way of life', what is an important prerequisite for parents who desire to instruct their children in Bible truth?
2. Read Deuteronomy 6:1–7.
   (a) What does the small word 'do' in this passage teach us about biblical instruction?
   (b) What does verse 7 in particular teach us about biblical instruction in the family?
3. Read Exodus 12:26–27. What principles can we learn from the Passover feast that help us to understand biblical instruction in the home?
4. Discuss each of the following in relation to biblical instruction in the home:
   (a) Leading the time of instruction.
   (b) Reading the Bible.
   (c) The importance of prayer.
   (d) The importance of singing.
   (e) The importance of memorization.
   (f) The importance of keeping a regular time.
   (g) The importance of variety.

FOR PERSONAL REFLECTION

5. As a parent, have you seriously considered the importance of your role in preparing your family for eternity? What practical measures do you actually take in this preparation?

Notes

1 **Alexander,** *Thoughts on Family Worship*, p. 1.
2 **Henry W. Holloman,** 'Basic biblical principles of Christian nurture and some considerations for their contextualization', in *Michigan Theological Journal*, vol. 1:1 (Spring 1990), p. 17 (electronic edition in Logos Library System). See also Deuteronomy 6:6–7; Joshua 24:15; Acts 18:26; 2 Timothy 1:5; 3:15.
3 Quoted by **Jonathan Lamb** in *Tough Minds, Tender Hearts* (IVP, 1997), p. 31.

Chapter 11

4 Remember that most of the Old Testament was written in the Hebrew language and with a Hebrew mindset. Furthermore, much of the New Testament (although written in Greek) also reflects this Hebrew mindset, since many of the New Testament authors were Hebrew in origin.

5 See **Allen P. Ross,** *Creation and Blessing: A Guide to the Study and Exposition of Genesis* (Grand Rapids: Baker, 1988), p. 349.

6 בָּרַךְ has the basic meaning 'to kneel' or 'to bless'.

7 **Alexander,** p. 52.

8 Ibid. p. 203.

9 **Susan Greenfield,** *The Human Brain: A Guided Tour* (Weidenfeld and Nicholson, 1997), p. 118.

10 **Holloman,** 'Basic biblical principles', p. 10.

11 In *The Subordinate Standards and Other Authoritative Documents of the Free Church of Scotland* (reprinted by William Blackwood & Sons Ltd, 1973), pp. 226–232.

12 **Daphne Spraggett** and **Jill Johnstone,** *Window on the World* (Carlisle: Paternoster, 2001).

13 For more information go to www.cefonline.com

14 **Alexander,** p. 194.

15 On this see **Alexander,** p. 236.

Select bibliography

Adams, Jay E., *Christian Living in the Home* (Presbyterian and Reformed Publishing Company, 1972).

Alexander, James W., *Thoughts on Family Worship*, 1847, and **Palmer, B. M.,** *The Family: In its Civil and Churchly Aspects*, 1876. Published together as one volume by Sprinkle Publications, 1991.

Christenson, Larry and Nordis, *The Christian Couple* (Bethany House Publishers, 1977).

Edwards, Brian and Barbara, *No Longer Two* (Epsom: Day One Publications, 1994).

James, John Angell, *A Help to Domestic Happiness* (Morgan, PA: Soli Deo Gloria Publications, 1995) (first published in 1833 by Frederick Westley and A. H. Davis).

Mack, Wayne A., *Strengthening Your Marriage* (Presbyterian and Reformed Publishing Company, 1977).

Mack, Wayne A., *Your Family God's Way* (Presbyterian and Reformed Publishing Company, 1991).

Marston, Paul, *God and the Family* (Eastbourne: Kingsway Publications, 1980).

Payne, Tony and Jensen, Philip D., *Pure Sex* (Matthias Media, 1998).

Richardson, John, *God, Sex, and Marriage: Guidance from 1 Corinthians 7* (MPA Books & St Mathias Press, 1995).

Scudder, Henry, *The Christian's Daily Walk* (Sprinkle Publications, 1984).

About Day One:

Day One's threefold commitment:

- To be faithful to the Bible, God's inerrant, infallible Word;
- To be relevant to our modern generation;
- To be excellent in our publication standards.

I continue to be thankful for the publications of Day One. They are biblical; they have sound theology; and they are relative to the issues at hand. The material is condensed and manageable while, at the same time, being complete—a challenging balance to find. We are happy in our ministry to make use of these excellent publications.

JOHN MACARTHUR, PASTOR-TEACHER, GRACE COMMUNITY CHURCH, CALIFORNIA

It is a great encouragement to see Day One making such excellent progress. Their publications are always biblical, accessible and attractively produced, with no compromise on quality. Long may their progress continue and increase!

JOHN BLANCHARD, AUTHOR, EVANGELIST AND APOLOGIST

Visit our website for more information and to request a free catalogue of our books.

www.dayone.co.uk

John Rogers—Sealed with blood
The story of the first Protestant
martyr of Mary Tudor's reign

TIM SHENTON,

160PP PAPERBACK

978-1-84625-084-2

John Rogers— sealed with blood
The story of the first Protestant martyr of Mary Tudor's reign

Tim Shenton

We in the west sorely need to craft a theology of martyrdom—it would put backbone into our proclamation and living, and help us remember brothers and sisters going through fiery trials even today in other parts of the world. Remembering men like John Rogers is a great help in the development of such a theology.

MICHAEL HAYKIN, PRINCIPAL AND PROFESSOR OF CHURCH HISTORY AND REFORMED SPIRITUALITY, TORONTO BAPTIST SEMINARY, TORONTO, ONTARIO

Tim Shenton is the head teacher of St Martin's School and an elder at Lansdowne Baptist Church, Bournemouth. He is married with two daughters. He has researched and written extensively on church history, specializing in the eighteenth and nineteenth centuries. Among his works published by Day One are *Forgotten heroes of Revival, Our perfect God, Opening up 1 Thessalonians* and an expositional commentary on the prophet Habakkuk.

'Tim Shenton has produced yet another well-documented, gripping biography of a real hero of faith—John Rogers (d. 1555), renowned biblical editor and first Marian martyr. Follow Rogers's fascinating career from Antwerp to Germany, and back again to England, where he was arrested, remained steadfast under intense interrogation, and paid the ultimate price for confessing Christ. This is a great book about an important epigone; hopefully, Rogers will no longer be marginalized! Highly recommended for teenagers and adults.'
—*JOEL R BEEKE, PURITAN REFORMED THEOLOGICAL SEMINARY, GRAND RAPIDS, MICHIGAN*

'Shenton weaves a brilliant tapestry from original sources and introduces the reader to many compelling and complex personalities. Well-proportioned in its emphasis, this history will be a vital contribution to studies of Protestant martyrs in Queen Mary's reign.'
—*RANDALL J. PEDERSON, CO-AUTHOR OF MEET THE PURITANS*